COLLABORATIVE
STRATEGIC PLANNING
IN HIGHER EDUCATION

Patrick Sanaghan

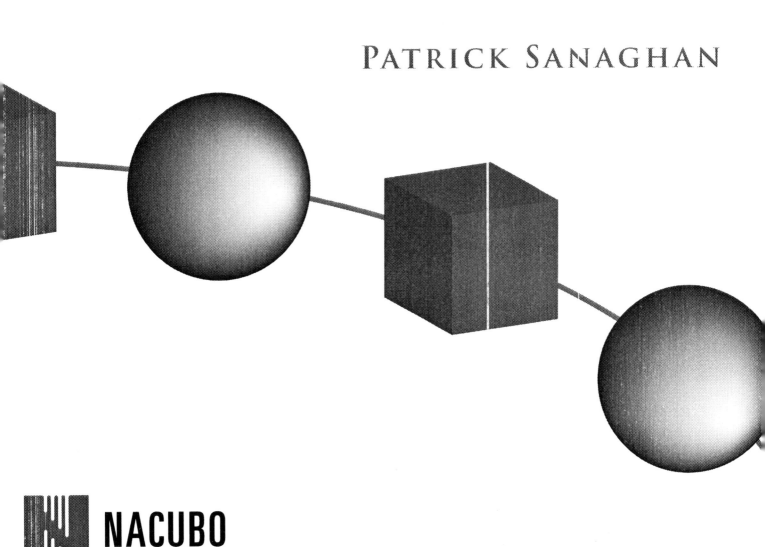

NACUBO

Library of Congress Cataloging-in-Publication Data

Sanaghan, Patrick.
  Collaborative strategic planning in higher education / by Patrick Sanaghan.
    p. cm.
  ISBN 978-1-56972-047-9
  1. Universities and colleges--United States--Planning. 2. Strategic planning--United States. I. Title.
  LB2341.S24 2009
  378.1'01--dc22
                    2008052982

Design by Colburnhouse

National Association of College and University Business Officers
Washington, DC
www.nacubo.org

Printed in the United States of America

Words of praise for

COLLABORATIVE STRATEGIC PLANNING IN HIGHER EDUCATION

"In *Collaborative Strategic Planning in Higher Education*, Pat Sanaghan effectively organizes and synthesizes more than 25 years of leadership, coordination, and facilitation of highly successful strategic planning engagements with multiple organizations and thousands of individuals. This work not only presents proven concepts and principles, it essentially creates a "how to" manual for effective strategic planning in higher education. Sanaghan's book is full of proven strategies, methods, and real world tools—enriched and strengthened with insights and actual examples of what does and doesn't work in our unique industry. While this work covers the subject from concept to implementation, it recognizes the unique differences and cultures that require customization and sensitivity at the institution level. This book is the next best thing to having Pat Sanaghan as a part of your staff."

Brett A. Dalton
Chief Financial Officer
Clemson University

"Given the increasing demand for scarce resources in higher education, presidents, facilitators, and planning committee chairs will find this book invaluable to strategic planning. Sanaghan hits home with real life examples that illustrate every step of the strategic planning process. This outstanding book should be on the shelf of every strategic planner."

Robert L. Lovitt
Executive Vice President for Finance and Administration
Texas A&M University—Corpus Christi

"Strategic planning in higher education is fraught with pitfalls—particularly in these challenging times. *Collaborative Strategic Planning in Higher Education* is full of innovative activities and approaches designed to overcome these obstacles and develop the creative space and shared commitment to move forward. I have successfully adopted many of the activities in this book in my own planning process, and I can say that both novices and experienced professionals will find good advice in these pages."

Clint Sidle
Director of the Roy H. Park Leadership Fellows Program at the Johnson School
Cornell University

"The collaborative undertone expressed throughout Patrick Sanaghan's new book points to the practical reality that higher education organizations can no longer operate in division-based silos. We must adopt a new dynamic that centers on a well-orchestrated entity of educators maximizing our financial, physical, and human resources. This book provides a fine foundation for planning and a wealth of practical suggestions to aid the process."

Dr. Jeffrey Pittman
Vice President for Student Services
Regent University

CONTENTS

ABOUT THE AUTHOR

Patrick Sanaghan, Ed.D., is the president of The Sanaghan Group, an organizational consulting firm that specializes in strategic planning, leadership development, executive team building, meeting facilitation, and leadership transitions. He has worked in more than 100 organizations and 60 campuses over the last 25 years and has taught strategic planning to more than 1,000 administrators in higher education.

Sanaghan speaks and writes frequently on leadership and strategic planning. He has written numerous articles and co-authored several books on strategic planning, high-performing teams, and change management. His most recent book, *Presidential Transitions*, was published by ACE/Praeger in 2007. He is at work on a book on exceptional leadership.

Clients of The Sanaghan Group have included The College of New Rochelle, Cornell University, DePaul University, Marywood University, Misercordia University, Saint Joseph's University, Shoreline Community College, and The University of the West Indies, as well as such corporate clients as Barclay Capital, Independence Blue Cross Insurance, PSE&G, The Parallax Hedge Fund, The Pennsylvania Ballet, IBM, Saudi Aramco, Shell Oil, and UNEXT. He serves on the boards of The Lopez-Low Foundation and The Wheeled Scotsman.

ACKNOWLEDGMENTS

Many past and present thinkers, theorists, and practitioners contributed to the creation of the Collaborative Strategic Planning (CSP) process. They include Ron Lippitt, who made many of his contributions to collaborative thinking in the 1960s and 1970s. I've drawn on his seminal work with large group meetings and use his model of creating a "preferred future" in planning. Marvin Weisbord and Sandra Janoff, co-creators of The Future Search methodology, deserve attention and respect as well.

Peter Senge, with his books *The Fifth Discipline* and *The Dance of Change* deserves mention, as do Dick Axelrod's *Terms of Engagement* and Robert W. Jacob's *Real Time Strategic Change*. All these authors are leading thinkers in the field of collaborative work. They have provided organization leaders, thinkers, and consultants with robust ideas, principles, and philosophies that are both deeply practical and humane.

On a personal note, Nancy Aronson, a wonderful friend and colleague, has contributed mightily to my knowledge about collaborative practices. Larry Goldstein, another colleague has been a great thought partner in my learning journey.

Having worked on scores of campuses throughout the United States and overseas, I've dealt with tough faculty, tough presidents, and tough issues. I've also had the privilege of working with great faculty, presidents, and administrators. All have contributed to the lessons learned and shared on these pages.

Once you have engaged campus stakeholders in crafting a planning process worthy of their commitment, you are well-positioned to draft a plan that will move your institution toward a shared, compelling vision. Welcome to the journey.

Patrick Sanaghan, Ed.D.
Doylestown, Pennsylvania

INTRODUCTION

Almost every college and university has a detailed strategic plan, typically a well-written one. Yet many strategic plans fall far short of their intended aspirations and outcomes.

Strategic planning—both in the corporate world and within higher education—tends to break down during implementation. In other words, writing the plan is the easy part; putting the plan into action proves much harder. Reasons for this may include an overly ambitious plan or one not based on solid data.

Within higher education, however, strategic planning falls short of its potential or simply fails for one main reason: The internal stakeholders feel no connection to the plan and therefore are not committed to its implementation. Often, people feel as if the plan is something done *to* or *for* them but not *with* them. They do not believe their ideas were heard because no one really attempted to solicit their opinions or discuss their concerns and hopes. Rarely do they receive strategic information to review, including the financial implications of proposed decisions.

These feelings of disconnectedness grow out of the way the strategic planning is typically conducted. *The process itself is the problem.* If campus stakeholders don't feel meaningfully involved and don't have the opportunity to share their ideas and aspirations, learn from others, and help influence the future goals and directions of the institution, they will not be committed to implementing the plan—no matter how well it is written.

To craft strategic plans that will enable their institutions to thrive in the future, campus leaders must learn how to connect with and engage stakeholders throughout the institution. They must put away the charts, numbers, matrixes, and all thoughts of a purely linear planning process. Nor can they rely on a visionary president to dream up an institutional future and then assume everyone on campus will buy into that same idea. Instead, we all must become "horizon thinkers" and look into the future together, with good information, diverse perspectives, shared values, and great hopes.

A Five-Phase Approach

This book outlines a simple, five-phase collaborative approach to strategic planning that has worked effectively on many campuses. Specifically, Collaborative Strategic Planning (CSP) refers to the disciplined and thoughtful process of meaningfully engaging relevant stakeholders in creating a shared future vision and goals for their institution.

The five phases are:
- **Phase I: Getting Organized.** Spearheaded by the president, this phase includes establishing a strategic planning task force, committing the resources necessary to support the process, and communicating the importance of the planning effort.
- **Phase II: Data Gathering and Engagement.** Face-to-face interaction, discussion, and dialogue with stakeholders all play a role during this stage of the planning task force's work.
- **Phase III: Making Sense of the Issues.** Based on the information gathered, the task force identifies several major strategic themes and develops a concept paper for each one.
- **Phase IV: Vision Conference.** This highly interactive, one-day meeting brings together stakeholders to discuss the concept papers and create a "preferred future."
- **Phase V: Goals Conference.** With input from key stakeholders, the planning task force creates a set of goals for each of the strategic themes explored during the vision conference. These strategic goals form the basis for an action plan and a detailed implementation plan.

You will find nothing brilliant or dramatically new about CSP. Much of it is common sense—and that may be its greatest strength. CSP is especially attentive to the process of planning—the way the planning process is designed, organized, and implemented. Without an effective process, a strategic plan will not be worth the great effort it takes to do well.

How This Book Is Organized

In the chapters that follow, you will find many creative, practical, and inclusive ways to engage stakeholders based on your institution's unique culture, goals, and needs. This is an important point: No "one model" approach can manage the diverse complexities and challenges of every campus. Your institution needs a customized approach.

The beauty of CSP is that you can tailor it to meet your needs, resources, and aspirations. Although most institutions that have done CSP have implemented the entire five-phase model, some have implemented only the two or three phases needed on their campus. In fact, because the framework and principles of CSP transcend campus politics, culture, and complexity, you can apply the process in a wide variety of situations and places. For instance, educational institutions have used it with technology implementations that required stakeholder buy-in, for self-studies in preparation for external accreditation, and for curriculum reviews and renewal with faculty.

Chapter 1 explains how collaborative strategic planning differs from other approaches your institution may have used in the past and describes the four steps essential to its success. Chapter 2 explores the concept of design and how it relates to and influences CSP by walking you through a collaborative planning activity in detail. This chapter also discusses the four elements of collaborative meetings: purpose, stakeholders, design, and logistics.

In Chapter 3 you'll learn the details of Phase I: Getting Organized. In many ways, this chapter is the heart of the book. It describes how the planning task force becomes educated about collaborative planning and then creates a disciplined process to engage the entire campus community.

Chapter 4 describes Phase II: Data Gathering and Engagement. It shows how the planning task force members actively engage stakeholders on campus through a series of interactive meetings aimed at generating ideas, identifying institutional strengths and weaknesses, and articulating institutional values.

Chapter 5 covers Phase III: Making Sense of the Issues. Rather than jumping to solutions before the complexities and issues are fully understood, this phase builds in time to discuss and think about the information generated during Phase II. This chapter also describes the creation of concept papers to summarize and clarify the strategic themes that emerge from the data-gathering exercises.

Chapter 6 covers Phase IV: Vision Conference. Involving both internal and external stakeholders, this event provides an opportunity for different groups (faculty, alumni, parents, students) to share their unique perspectives of the institution's future. The participative event culminates with stakeholders creating a shared picture of the institution's future.

Chapter 7 describes Phase V: Goals Conference, where the planning task force and other relevant stakeholders come together to identify a set of strategic goals that need to be implemented to achieve the shared vision articulated during Phase IV. In addition to creating an action plan with specific objectives for each set of strategic goals, the participants identify accountability points (who will do what).

Chapter 8 discusses the implementation phase of the collaborative planning process—where real planning begins. It offers specific models, timelines, and frameworks for monitoring accountability for the entire plan. For a real-world perspective, Chapter 9 summarizes lessons learned about the anticipated hurdles and challenges facing any planning effort.

Following a list of recommended resources, the five appendices provide additional information on how to use CSP for the greatest effect. They include an executive summary that can help explain the five-phase planning process to presidents, trustees, faculty, and others; two examples of concept papers; a planning audit that assesses an institution's capacity to plan before it undertakes the process; and several techniques for fostering collaboration.

Unique Benefits

Collaborative strategic planning does everything that regular strategic planning does: It creates a compelling vision and goals, identifies the financial impacts of decisions, uses data to inform dialogue and decisions, identifies campus priorities, and creates the nuts-and-bolts action plans necessary for implementation.

In addition, CSP contributes to the institution in several distinctive ways. The five-phase process:

- **Improves or builds organizational capacity.** Once campus stakeholders have experienced and used collaborative methodologies they are better able to facilitate effective meetings, distill meaning from complex data, understand the budget, constructively challenge thinking about institutional issues, solve complex problems, and teach others in an engaging and responsive manner.

- **Consciously solicits the ideas of diverse stakeholders.** As participants begin to understand the complexities, challenges, and strengths of the institution from other people's perspectives, the institution itself grows smarter. When more people understand more, they become actively engaged in influencing and crafting a future worthy of their commitment; no one has to push or cajole them to move toward the future.

- **Encourages a larger perspective of the institution's future.** Participants move from their own organizational silos (such as faculty, student life, or finance) and see the campus through others' eyes. When stakeholders experience the interconnectedness of issues, problems, and opportunities, they discover their common aspirations rather than get stuck in their differences.

- **Improves the quality of the decisions made through a strategic planning process.** One reason to engage in strategic planning is to make more informed decisions that will enable you to effectively meet the challenges of the future. With more people involved in the planning process, decision makers obtain more information (such as financial, branding, and demographic data) from diverse perspectives. Given this richer database, stakeholders are better informed *before* they make their decisions. They are able to look at the whole institution rather than its parts (for example, business school or student life) and begin to understand the long-term impacts of their proposed decisions.

- **Builds or enhances institutional trust.** Trust is the most fragile yet enduring element in organizational life. Without trust, a president—no matter how brilliant or hard working—cannot lead. And when leadership is not trusted, the institution stalls and remains in neutral. Typically, when trust breaks down between faculty and administration, anger prevails, conflict arises over every little issue, and ideas are judged not on their merit but on who has proposed them. In contrast, a college or university that enjoys a high level of trust can accomplish great things. One way to build trust is to use an open, inclusive, and participative planning process.

CSP is not a miracle methodology. Still, its guiding principles of inclusion, transparency (especially about the budget), and participation enable campus stakeholders to begin talking about sensitive issues, to discuss what truly matters, to resolve some differences, and to even rebuild relationships.

chapter 1

LAYING THE FOUNDATION

Although it arrives at the same destination as other planning approaches, collaborative strategic planning (CSP) follows a different path along the way. Eight characteristics of CSP set it apart from—and make it more effective than—other approaches.

Specifically, CSP encourages:

- **Meaningful engagement of institutional stakeholders.** Rather than using impersonal questionnaires and surveys, CSP engages people through face-to-face interaction and personal discussions.

- **Transparency of information.** All relevant stakeholders have access to the information gathered, which belongs to the institution and not some small, powerful group. This openness—especially regarding financial information—translates into no secrets and no clandestine decision-making processes.

- **Diversity of ideas.** Collaborative planning assumes that everyone can contribute to the process and explicitly creates opportunities for stakeholders to share their various perspectives, experiences, and views.

- **Ownership of the planning process—especially its outcomes.** Internal stakeholders feel committed to implementing the strategic plan because they put their resources, skills, wisdom, and knowledge into creating it. Although you may use a consultant to facilitate the planning process, his or her role is to build the capacity of internal stakeholders and pay attention to the process—not the content—of the plan. The internal stakeholders take full responsibility for organizing, facilitating, data gathering, decision making, and making sense of the issues.

- **Reflection and making sense of the issues.** Often, people in organizations make quick decisions and take action long before they fully understand a particular issue or challenge. In contrast, CSP builds in time to reflect and make sense of emerging issues, institutional values, and the complexity of challenges. During the data-gathering phase, new information surfaces, challenges become more apparent, and stakeholders clarify their aspirations.

- **Discovery and learning.** CSP has no hidden agenda and doesn't try to steer stakeholders toward some anticipated or predetermined outcome. Rather, as the process unfolds, stakeholders learn how to create shared aspirations, visions, and goals for their institution.

- **An external perspective.** One danger of planning is listening to yourself too much. In other words, institutions can become trapped in their own way of thinking about issues and perhaps a bit too self-referential. Too inwardly focused on information and details, they may be unwilling to take an honest, tough look at themselves. CSP pays explicit attention to the external realities that campus stakeholders, especially the leadership, must factor into their decision making. For example, what trends and issues are impacting higher education? What are best practices for student life, faculty teaching, and financial allocation models? What are the implications of changing and emerging technologies?

- **Community building and connections.** Planning is all about people: their hopes and aspirations, their values and principles, what matters to them, what they want the institution to become, even what they feel. But building connections with the people throughout a campus doesn't mean taking some strange, touchy feely approach to planning or foisting silly games or techniques on people to promote a false sense of community. Instead, CSP creates opportunities for open dialogue and meaningful involvement. When people's ideas are valued and respected, when information is transparent and shared across boundaries, positive things happen. People begin to understand one another's perspectives, share their aspirations, and engage together in "informed dreaming."

Of course, you don't announce upfront that "We are here to build a sense of community and connection on this campus." People (especially faculty) would run for the hills. Community building is an outcome of good planning that consciously involves diverse stakeholders in a transparent process about what truly matters on their campus.

Four Steps to Success

Because CSP takes a different approach to strategic planning, it's important to highlight the four steps essential to its ultimate success.

1. **Appoint a credible Planning Task Force (PTF).** This task force will guide the process from the beginning to the end, so its composition will make or break the planning effort. People will judge the potential effectiveness of the planning task force based on its members' capacity, knowledge, and talents.

    All task force members must have excellent reputations and be willing to work hard. They must be both thinkers and doers. With CSP, the task force members—not the consultants—do most of the heavy lifting. Most planning processes have an oversight or governing mechanism to provide counsel; in CSP, the planning task force does this and more. (See Chapter 3 for more information on the PTF.)

FACILITATOR'S TIP

Develop a delegation plan for the co-chairs of the Planning Task Force to help them clarify their primary job responsibilities and determine what can be temporarily delegated to others. One university, for example, relieved a faculty member of one teaching course for an academic year, giving him more time to co-chair the task force.

2. **Ensure the president engages with and participates in the planning process.** The president cannot be seen as driving the process or persuading stakeholders to agree with a particular vision for the institution. Nor can the president appear far removed from the process, which communicates a possible lack of interest in or commitment to the planning results. Instead, the president must occupy the space between these extremes and be a facilitative leader willing to let the strategic planning task force do its work. In this role, the president should:

   - Communicate to the entire campus, with interest and enthusiasm, that the strategic planning process will be inclusive, participative, transparent, and vitally important to the future of the institution. This is usually done at a kick-off meeting that signals the beginning of the planning process, possibly a convocation or special event at the beginning of the academic year. Of course, the president's support must be visible and authentic throughout the planning process, not just at its start.

   - Attend the training sessions at the beginning of the process to learn about collaborative practices. The president's attendance signals to PTF members that they are undertaking important work worthy of their time and commitment.

   - Talk about and discuss the planning process at numerous meetings with alumni, parents, students, community members, faculty, and so forth. In addition to communicating about the planning process, the president needs to listen at these meetings. Stakeholders will share many perceptions, concerns, hopes, and aspirations—all strategic information.

   - Participate in several data-gathering meetings conducted by the PTF. The president will not only learn about stakeholder ideas but also can emphasize the value that participation brings to the process.

   - Relieve the PTF co-chairs of some of their daily job responsibilities, if possible. Serving as a co-chair will take a considerable amount of time and attention; it is not a part-time position that can be responsibly executed within a couple of hours a month. Co-chairs, for example, need to talk with the outside planning consultants to strategize unforeseen challenges and meet with PTF members to provide encouragement, participate in problem solving, and listen to what has been learned.

   - Meet regularly with the PTF co-chairs for progress updates.

3. **Keep the board informed about the planning process.** Ensure that trustees understand the rationale behind the collaborative planning process and the intended outcomes before the planning process begins. Ideally, the president—with support from any outside consultants—should explain how the planning process will look and feel. To further board members' understanding, it's helpful for them to actually experience a collaborative planning exercise such as the Future Timeline or The Carousel SWOT Analysis (see Chapter 3). Every time the board meets subsequently, the president should report on the progress of the planning process and the issues emerging from it. If possible, the co-chairs should also meet with the board.

FACILITATOR'S TIP

Organize several planning sessions around the president's calendar, to ensure he or she can attend. This can greatly improve attendance, especially at participative data-gathering meetings. People not only like being around the president but also feel their own efforts are worthwhile when the president takes the time to participate as well.

Although appointing trustees to serve on the PTF may sound like a good idea, it simply doesn't work well in reality. The task force's dynamics change dramatically when its membership includes a trustee; conversations are different when the other participants realize that a governing member of the institution is in the room with them. For example, other members of the task force tend to avoid discussing difficulties when a board member is present. Or some PTF members may lobby harder for their particular viewpoint because they have the rare opportunity of influencing a board member.

4. **Create a common language about planning.** Agree on the definitions of several words before you begin planning. This might sound simple; it isn't. During discussions, many people throw around planning terms—such as *vision, goals,* and *strategies*—and assume everyone else both understands and agrees on the terms' definitions. Massive confusion may result if you don't reach agreement before engaging in discussions, making decisions, or communicating information to stakeholders.

As an example, one university engaged in strategic planning for 14 years with nothing to show for the efforts. Three different presidents had tried to get things moving but were unable to reach consensus with the faculty. During one meeting with 40 faculty members, discussions focused on the barriers to moving forward, including the needs for financial transparency, stakeholder engagement, and a faculty voice. But the biggest takeaway from the meeting was that no one could agree on the definition of *consensus.* Faculty members used the word frequently yet had a wide variety of opinions about what it actually meant.

Collaborative strategic planning strives for a consensus mentality, characterized by open discussion and dialogue, careful listening by everyone involved, transparency of information, and the willingness to listen to different ideas and perspectives. Before engaging in CSP, therefore, these faculty members needed to agree on a working definition of consensus (which, incidentally, took six months).

This rather dramatic example is not intended to lay the blame for a stalled process on faculty. Many university presidents and other campus leaders often speak of consensus during speeches and discussions with faculty and staff. What exactly do they mean by the term? The definition varies widely. Clarify everyone's understanding of consensus long before getting to the point in the strategic planning process where tough, complex decisions need to be made.

William G. Ouchi, author of *Theory Z,* offers one potential definition. Ouchi believes that consensus has been reached when all members of a group can agree on a single solution or decision when each person can say:

- I believe that you understand my point of view.
- I believe that I understand your point of view.
- Whether or not I prefer the decision, I will support it because it was reached openly and fairly.

Note that Ouchi talks about *understanding* one another's perspective; he doesn't say *agreeing* with it.

COMING TO TERMS

Here are suggested definitions of common planning terms that may work for your institution. If they don't, that's fine—just be sure to come up with agreed-upon definitions before moving forward with the planning process.

- **Vision:** A description of a desired future state. The best visions are vivid, compelling, and well-understood and build on the institution's strengths and values.

- **Values:** The core beliefs and guiding principles that govern daily behavior, communication, decision making, and leadership within an organization. These are considered non-negotiable.

- **Mission:** Articulates the institution's purpose and the major activities in which it is engaged. By incorporating its particular values, an institution differentiates itself from other organizations engaged in similar activities.

- **Goals:** Large-scale efforts that, when accomplished, move the organization closer to its vision. Effective goals are subject to assessment.

- **Strategy:** A particular approach in pursuit of an organization's vision, usually in support of one or more specific goals.

- **Strategic Plan:** The narrative map that communicates where an organization wants to go and identifies how it intends to get there.

- **Outputs:** The services or products provided by an institution. Relevant measures related to outputs typically focus on efficiency (for example, the number of annual graduates).

- **Outcomes:** An organization's impact on the external environment or the value it provides through its products or services. Relevant measures related to outcomes typically focus on effectiveness (for example, the percentage of students obtaining a job in their educational field or admitted to medical school).

BASIC PRINCIPLES

As a preparation for collaborative strategic planning (CSP), this chapter explains the key principles behind it.

The Concept of Design

Effective and engaging meetings do not happen simply by chance. You can't put a group of smart people in a room and hope something wonderful happens. The collaborative planner must develop a design mentality and consciously plan and facilitate each meeting.

The term *design* refers to the creative process of planning and facilitating a set of activities that move a group successfully and transparently toward conscious goals. The concept crops up repeatedly in our daily lives. For example, if you wanted to give a birthday party for a close friend, you might invite specific guests who are close to the birthday boy or girl, arrange for upbeat music, plan some fun activities, decorate your home with balloons and other festive items, and order a birthday cake. You'd carefully and intentionally plan all of the details (such as how many people will attend and where the party will take place) to achieve your desired outcome of celebrating your friend's birthday.

Now imagine that you had the unfortunate task of planning a memorial service for the same friend. Although many of the same elements from the birthday party might be present, you would organize, or design, them very differently. The same people might attend—but their dress would be somber, not festive. The music would be subdued rather than upbeat. You might serve food but, rather than being a centerpiece for the gathering, it would be for sustenance only. The decorations would be conservative and respectful, the colors muted rather than bright.

Same friend, same people attending—but, because of the circumstances, the two events would be designed and organized differently. Similarly, every collaborative meeting has myriad details to think through and organize based on the desired outcome.

Four Elements of Interactive Meetings

Four elements come into play when you want to create interactive and participative meetings. They are:

1. **Purpose.** What do you want to accomplish at a particular meeting? To zero in on your purpose, it may help to answer these questions:
    - Am I trying to prioritize a set of planning recommendations?
    - Am I deciding something or seeking input from participants?
    - Do I want to share information with people and then solicit feedback?
    - Do I have a problem I need help in solving, or do I want to provide a solution and test its soundness with others?
    - Do I want to openly discuss a sensitive topic or gather data about it?
    - Do I want participants to share their accomplishments or their concerns?

    The answer to each question would point to different purposes. For instance, deciding something is different than discussing. Prioritizing is different than discussing a sensitive topic. Each of these different purposes would call for a different set of activities or designs. Communicate your purpose(s) to the invited participants before they attend the planning meeting. This not only communicates transparency but also enables participants to prepare for what will take place.

    As you think about the outcomes you want to achieve, also think of the process goals you want to accomplish. In other words, how do you want people to feel about the experience? You might, for instance, want to make sure people feel as if their contributions were valued, that they had a chance to truly participate and influence the ideas of others, and that the meeting created a sense of community. The facilitator doesn't need to communicate the process goals to attendees but should think them through carefully.

    Once you have determined the meeting's purpose, you can begin thinking about the other three key elements to collaborative meetings. Without a clearly understood and articulated purpose, everything else will suffer.

2. **Stakeholders.** After defining the purpose(s), ask, "Who needs to be at this planning meeting or series of meetings to accomplish the purpose(s)?" Your answer will identify those who have a stake in the meeting (such as faculty or students) and whose participation is essential to accomplishing the purposes of the meeting. In short, think about those individuals or groups who could either help you with their participation or hurt you if they aren't invited.

    If you want to solve a complex problem on campus, for instance, you may want participants who have some experience with the problem, could be affected by the problem, or can provide creative ideas and approaches to the problem. These may be three distinct stakeholder groups. Or, to have a full conversation about campus-wide communication, you would have to identify representatives from a variety of stakeholder groups, such as students, staff, administrators, faculty, and communication experts.

Every campus has scores of potential stakeholders. The challenge is to determine what stakeholders must be involved in a particular meeting. Many institutions fall into the trap of inviting everyone to everything rather than being conscious and intentional about the attendee list. But if the same set of players always gets together to solve institutional problems, their view will be narrow and unchanging.

3. **Design.** As noted above, focus on organizing the meeting so that it realizes your intended outcomes. Think through the set of questions related to determining purpose and figure out the kinds of activities that will help engage participants and get the job done.

   For a reality check, bounce your ideas off several colleagues. Explain what you want to accomplish, who will attend, and how you intend to achieve the intended results. Your colleagues will help you identify the strengths and weaknesses of your design so you can better prepare for the meeting. Also inform the president of what design or set of designs you'll use, so there won't be any surprises.

4. **Logistics.** Logistics refers to all the physical things that help support the discussions, dialogues, and learning experiences that the meeting is designed to produce. These range from the space and set-up of the meeting room to which items participants may need to complete their work.

   Before the meeting occurs, visit the room you will be using to get a feel for its strengths and weaknesses. A diagram is rarely helpful. Because many collaborative activities use flipchart paper, look for adequate wall space on which to post the paper. Many meeting rooms on campuses have beautiful pictures, sconces, curtains, and candleholders on the walls; hanging paper in such rooms is difficult.

   Also ensure you have enough space for people to feel comfortable moving around. Collaborative activities, which are designed for maximum interaction and participation, encourage a lot of movement. You can always make a large room smaller by rearranging flipcharts and chairs but a small, cramped room can't be enlarged. Bigger is almost always better.

   On the day of the meeting, show up early so you'll have time to fix anything that may seem wrong with the physical arrangement and other details. Here's why: We once had a meeting scheduled for more than 100 faculty members. When we asked to look over the room beforehand, the president replied, "You will love the room. It's large and can hold almost 200 people. There's not enough time to see it because it is way across campus and we have a lot to do today."

   We never saw the room, much to our chagrin. When we showed up the next day to facilitate the meeting, we entered a large faculty dining room with six beautiful but large pillars that blocked everyone's view. The room was a great place to eat—but not to meet.

The Rule of Four

When designing collaborative meetings, one theory of group development and interaction is especially helpful to keep in mind. It's called the Rule of Four. According to this rule, about four or five people will dominate the discussion in almost every group numbering between 10 and 50 people. This small number of assertive and verbal people—not necessarily the smartest ones in the group—will do 80 percent of the talking!

Most people who have participated in an ongoing meeting such as a faculty senate, administrative council, or steering committee have experienced this rule. It thrives within higher education, for many reasons. For one, faculty members often have a special position in campus meetings and take full advantage of it. A few curmudgeons can easily take over a meeting. Also, when you have different levels of power (president, faculty, vice presidents, students) in a room, an individual's level can greatly influence his or her participation. Similarly, older people tend to dominate discussions that also include younger people, and participants perceived as experts in a particular area tend to share their knowledge more than listening to others.

The goal of the collaborative planner is not to shut down the four or five dominant personalities but to neutralize their impact on a group. To hear all the voices in the room, not just a few, use small groups of six to eight people to gather data and diagnose problems, help decide next steps, build agreement, and distill meaning from information and discussions. The smaller the group, the more likely more people are to speak up.

By the way, people who tend to dominate a meeting or group, like to be in charge, or prefer positions of power dislike smaller groups. They realize that they cannot control what is going on, cannot bully others into agreement, and cannot hold the stage when others in a small group are highly engaged and participative.

Proven Planning Designs

Remembering the Rule of Four throughout the planning process will improve the quality of the interactions and effectiveness of your meetings. To provide a head start, this book describes many collaborative designs that have already factored in the rule. You'll also find that these planning designs, which have proven effective on scores of campuses:

- **Are transparent.** Participants can clearly see and understand what is taking place during the meeting; there are no hidden agendas or manipulated purposes. If a meeting will result in a decision, the participants agree in advance on the rules for making the decision.
- **Enable participants to manage their own work.** These activities are not driven by outside experts or leaders. Participants take responsibility for organizing themselves, sharing information, and distilling meaning from their work.

FACILITATOR'S TIP

Develop your own list of items for every collaborative meeting. You might, for example, always want to have:

- Plenty of flipcharts and easels
- Dozens of magic markers in different colors
- Masking tape or large Post-it sheets
- Computer connections
- Paper and pens
- Moveable and comfortable chairs
- Plenty of wall space on which to post papers
- Portable microphones

- **Use and respect different learning styles.** Most meetings are driven by people who love information, facts, and structure. Unfortunately, most meetings are also unproductive because different participants want different things. Some seek a lot of interaction and dialogue, while others want to be inspired. Some want to use their imaginations to envision possibilities, and still others prize data and information. No one style is right. They are all needed to contribute effectively to the meeting's purposes.

- **Promote maximum participation and interaction.** By using small groups, these designs create opportunities for participants to contribute meaningfully; neutralize the impact of dominating or powerful individuals; and allow quiet, even shy, people to be heard.

- **Build community and connections.** Although task- and outcome-driven, the designs pay attention to process, or how things are accomplished during the meeting. Different group structures, open communication, and democratic principles combine to nurture positive relationships among participants. Participants feel connected to one another when they believe they are making a contribution to the institution and learning together. They also gain confidence in their ability to solve complex campus problems.

Start small if you are unfamiliar with these types of activities. Each planning design is marked either as being easy to execute, requiring moderate skill to facilitate, or being more challenging to do. Most of the designs are easy or moderate; even the few challenging ones don't require expert facilitation but rather careful attention to logistics and to moving people constructively toward the outcome of the activity.

Let's walk through one classic collaborative planning design that's easy to implement and execute. More important, it reveals a great deal about collaborative practices. We'll look at the design's elements as well as the thinking behind them.

The Cascading Agreement Design
Level of Difficulty: Easy
Estimated Time: 45 to 50 Minutes

Assume you've gathered 24 diverse individuals to discuss ways to improve campus morale. You're holding this meeting because, as the planning process has evolved, you've learned that some stakeholders do not feel valued. Moreover, a recent survey conducted by the HR department clearly indicates low morale on campus. Instead of waiting until the planning process has run its course, the president wants to tackle the issue and gather ideas on how to quickly improve morale.

HELPFUL HINTS

Keep these suggestions in mind when using the planning designs outlined in this book.

Work with a co-facilitator. Having a partner provides you with an additional set of eyes in the meeting and someone with whom to share the planning and logistics work. Plus, when formulating ideas, two heads are usually better than one.

Be prepared. Review the designs carefully, and make sure you have dealt with the four essential elements of a collaborative meeting: purpose, stakeholders, design, and logistics.

Do a dry run. To gain experience and confidence, try the activities first with a group of trusted colleagues.

Beware the rabbit ears. When you try a design that people are not familiar with, you may hear grumbling from curmudgeons in the group. (For instance, "We can all talk together in the large group; we don't need this small group stuff" or "What is all this touchy-feely stuff anyway?") Resist the temptation to react too quickly—like a rabbit—to respond to the muttered complaints. Calmly remind participants that the designs have been successfully tested by thousands of people on scores of other campuses.

Given the size of the group (24 participants), start by creating eight groups of three. In such a small group, there's no place to hide: All three members must participate. In larger groups of six or eight, one or two people can easily disappear during a discussion dominated by the most verbal participants.

Your room might look like this:

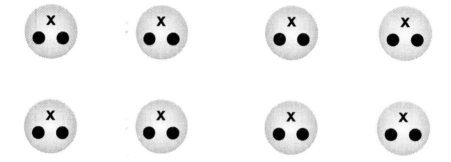

Facilitator's Directions

— Clarify the purpose of the meeting upfront. For example: "We are gathered here today to look at ways we can further improve campus morale. We want and need your ideas, and we want to hear from everyone." Explain that the planning design has four specific steps—but don't tell participants more than that. If you walk them through all four steps upfront, they will want to get to the end as fast as possible. In the race to the finish, you'd lose great ideas and provocative conversation.

— *(Step 1: Create)* Ask each group of three to brainstorm eight to 10 ways to improve campus morale. Emphasize that the quantity of ideas is important, so participants shouldn't be judgmental in this phase of the meeting design.

— Offer some suggestions to give participants an idea of what you are asking (for instance, offer free parking, have lunch with the president, and develop employee recognition programs). Ask each group to appoint someone to record the ideas, then give the trios about seven or eight minutes to work.

— *(Step 2: Condense)* Ask each group to reduce its list to the top three ideas generated during brainstorming. Explain that this step requires discipline and rigor in deciding what three ideas would best improve campus morale. Allocate three to five minutes for this task. If you give more time, people tend to debate, hold on to their ideas, and talk too much. The tight timeframe gently prods them to produce the best ideas.

Be on guard for clustering ideas or merging several ideas into one detailed recommendation. For example, "We should provide employee-of-the-month awards, along with a monetary reward, and have the president present these at an employee lunch" actually contains four ideas.

Initially, the eight groups will have generated 60 to 70 ways to improve campus morale. Now, they have whittled down their lists to the top 24 ideas. They will reduce the lists again in the next step.

— *(Step 3: Collaborate)* Ask each trio to connect with another trio, creating four groups of six participants.

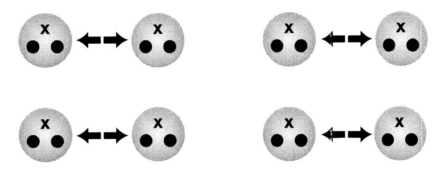

— The task now is to share each group's three best ideas and generally agree on the three best for the larger group. Encourage people to look for common themes but not cluster recommendations or engage in debate. Give them 10 to 12 minutes for this step.

— *(Step 4: Communicate)* After each group has agreed on its three best ideas, capture those recommendations on a flipchart in full view of all participants. Take one idea from each group of six, using a round-robin approach. Avoid taking all the ideas first from Group 1 and then from Group 2; by the time you get to Group 3, they may feel as if they have nothing new or meaningful to share. Make as many rounds as necessary to record all the ideas on the flipchart.

At this stage, your list might look like the flip chart here:

— Use a multi-voting technique, such as Las Vegas Voting (See Appendix A) to decide which ideas are the best. This simple prioritization process is completely transparent in its implementation. Give each participant five sticky dots (found at any stationary or office supply store). Explain that these dots represent votes. Participants can place their votes next to the ideas on the master list they believe are the best. They can weigh their votes any way they'd like. For example, they can place five dots on one idea, put two votes on one idea and three on another, or use one vote for each of five different ideas.

HOW TO IMPROVE CAMPUS MORALE
1. Have campus-wide picnics or events twice a year
2. Establish an employee recognition program
3. Establish "chews and chats" with the president to discuss issues of importance to employees
4. Have the president visit the monthly faculty senate meetings
5. Have "dress down" Fridays during the summer months
6. Create an ombudsman position so an impartial party can review grievances
7. Organize a special faculty meeting to discuss the issue and create specific recommendations for the president
8. Bring in outside experts to teach us how to improve morale
9. Appoint a "climate coordinator"
10. Have the president and provost be more visible on campus

As the participants come up to the flipchart and vote for their favorite ideas, you'll soon see priorities emerging on the list.

Your list may look like this:

HOW TO IMPROVE CAMPUS MORALE
1. Have campus-wide picnics or events twice a year√√√√√
2. Establish an employee recognition program √√√√√√√√√√√√
3. Establish "chews and chats" with the president to discuss issues of importance to employees√√√√√√√√√√√
4. Have the president visit the monthly faculty senate meetings√√√√
5. Have "dress down" Fridays during the summer months√√
6. Create an ombudsman position so an impartial party can review grievances√√√√√√
7. Organize a special faculty meeting to discuss the issue and create specific recommendations for the president√√√
8. Bring in outside experts to teach us how to improve morale√√
9. Appoint a "climate coordinator" √√√
10. Have the president and provost be more visible on campus√√√√√√√√√√√√√√

It is apparent to everyone that #2, #3, and #10 have the most votes.

Schedule

Introductions, welcome, and purposes	10 minutes
Trios brainstorm ideas	10 minutes
Trios agree on their three best ideas	5 minutes
Small groups work together and agree on the best ideas	10 minutes
Facilitator records ideas in full view	10 minutes
Las Vegas Voting (optional)	5 minutes
TOTAL	50 minutes

A diagnostic look at the Cascading Agreement design uncovers several collaborative principles.

- Starting with groups of three encourages full participation. Small groups are almost always the best way to go.
- The first step (Create) allows people to generate ideas without fear of judgment. This usually yields better ideas because participants don't censure themselves. Higher education tends to feature a lot of criticism, usually under the guise of being rigorous and disciplined. Such an academic approach can stifle creativity, while suspending judgment initially can encourage creativity.
- The second step (Condense) encourages conversation and disciplined thinking and begins to put some reasonable boundaries around what is possible. A tight timeframe keeps people moving toward outcomes rather than becoming bogged down in debate.
- The third step (Collaborate) encourages discussion and sharing of ideas; participants must listen to each other and work together to accomplish the task. It also shows that collaboration can happen in a short period of time.
- The summary piece of the design (Communicate) gathers all the ideas from the groups of six. Everything is transparent; the facilitator has no agenda. The facilitator's role is to structure a process that meets an intended outcome (a quality list of ideas). Participants experience group collaboration and, almost always, produce a product they feel proud about.
- Las Vegas Voting gives everyone the same number of votes to use as they see fit. No debate bogs down the meeting, and no one—not even the president—can control the outcome. The process is transparent to all.

Transparency is not only critical to collaborative work but also helps build trust in the planning process itself. The outcome of the Cascading Agreement design and any other collaborative design cannot be predetermined. Given a clear task, the participants will decide the outcome.

chapter 3

PHASE I—
GETTING ORGANIZED

Typically, Phase I of collaborative strategic planning (CSP) will take about two months to complete. Because they set the stage for all that will follow, the steps in this phase all require thoughtful consideration before proceeding. Here's how to begin.

Establish the Planning Task Force

The composition of the Planning Task Force (PTF) will make or break the entire planning process. Others will judge the meaningfulness, integrity, and worthiness of the process based on the people who serve on the PTF.

Ideally, the president should appoint two highly credible co-chairs—preferably a respected faculty member and a high-level administrator (such as the chief financial officer or vice president of enrollment). The choice of co-chairs will communicate volumes about how important the planning process is to the institution and its potential for success.

Like the co-chairs, the other members of the task force need to set the standard for excellence and leadership competency. Choose people with high credibility on campus (or within their department or division) and with solid reputations for being good thinkers as well as hard workers. Aim for a task force with between 20 and 30 members; working with a larger group (more than 50 members) presents challenges that can distract the task force from the planning process itself.

When selecting members of the PTF:

- Choose people who reflect the diversity of the institution. Include faculty, staff, administrators, and members of both genders.
- Avoid many of the "usual suspects"—the people who are in the institution's inner circle or always asked to sit on task forces and committees. Although you can include some of these people, they shouldn't represent a majority of the PTF membership. Make a point to recruit individuals who have high credibility on campus but are rarely asked to participate in institutional initiatives.

A CHAIR WITH CREDIBILITY

In the early 1990s, a large department at Cornell University decided to implement a collaborative planning process. The first task was to identify a highly credible candidate to chair the process, and the name of Dr. Keith Kennedy immediately came up. A bit of investigation revealed that Dr. Kennedy was Cornell's provost emeritus. At 80 years of age, he was immensely respected, even loved, for his contributions to the university, his character, and his intelligence.

When we met with Dr. Kennedy and the senior vice president to ask him about chairing the task force, the dialogue proved both interesting and rigorous. His passion for Cornell shone brightly. Several days later he agreed to chair the task force under two conditions. First, he wanted the final say on the composition of the task force's membership. Second, all information and decision making had to be completely transparent.

With everyone in agreement, the department had the most credible person on campus heading up its planning task force. Recruiting additional members from among the faculty and others on campus proved easy. Virtually everyone asked to serve on the task force said, "If Keith Kennedy is the chair, I know this will make a real difference to Cornell."

- Include informal leaders—people who may not have an impressive-sounding title but wield influence among their peers. Naming informal leaders to the PTF shows that collaborative planning differs from other types of strategic planning.
- Consider using the recommended mix of 60 percent faculty and 40 percent staff and administrators. Without faculty commitment, involvement, and buy-in to the planning process, it will fail. By making faculty the majority of PTF members, you give them the opportunity to express their opinions, articulate their aspirations, and meaningfully influence the direction of the planning process.
- Include one or two well-known curmudgeons—people who have a skeptical attitude about almost everything and willingly share their observations with others. These skeptics help provide rigor and credibility to the process because they typically have no problem speaking the truth regardless of who is in the room. They will ask tough questions, openly test decisions and theories, and ground the planning process in reality. (Note: More than two curmudgeons on a PTF will bog down the process.)
- Ensure the president's cabinet or senior team is well-represented because they will have responsibility for implementing the final plan. The cabinet needs to influence the discussions, provide their perspectives, and understand the issues. The cabinet's presence also communicates the institution's commitment, giving more credibility to the planning process.
- Identify several members who have the knowledge and expertise to serve as the communications team for the planning process. At least one should be a mid- or high-level technology administrator.
- Spell out exactly what the role and level of participation will be for every member of the PTF so no one will later be surprised by the work involved.

Determine the Calendar of Planning Events

Once assembled, the task force should develop a realistic schedule for the year-long planning process. On most campuses, the first two weeks and the last two weeks of each semester are too busy to accommodate any planning meetings or activities. The most important dates to establish are those for the vision conference (Phase IV) and the goals conference (Phase V).

Here's a sample calendar:

October	November/December	January	April	May
2-day Training Session for PTF	Data Gathering and Engagement	Making Sense of the Issues	Vision Conference	Goals Conference

Develop a Communication Process

The PTF needs to create an agile, transparent communication process that will keep all interested stakeholders fully informed about planning events, emerging issues, and the information generated throughout the planning process. In fact, campus-wide communication tends to improve overall when collaborative planning takes place; stakeholders come to expect clear, transparent, and honest information sharing within the institution even after the process has concluded.

Face-to-face meetings with stakeholders are the most effective way to keep people informed and engaged. These might take the form of "chews and chats" (see Chapter 4), where task force members convene brief meetings throughout the campus to communicate planning progress and solicit input.

Consider establishing two Web sites: one for campus stakeholders and another just for PTF members. Any stakeholder who wants to know how things are going with the planning process should have access to the campus site, which should have the capacity to solicit ideas and feedback from stakeholders. (This information should go directly to the PTF members.) The internal PTF Web site is meant for task force members only. It provides a vehicle for discussion; a place to post meeting minutes, summaries, and drafts of white papers on specific themes and issues; and a means of reviewing meeting logistics.

One caution: Do not depend solely on technology to keep stakeholders informed and solicit feedback. To reach a broader base of stakeholders, use additional vehicles (such as print and face-to-face meetings) for communication and interaction.

Train the Planning Task Force

To create a good beginning for the planning process, all PTF members must participate in a two-day training session. It features a series of collaborative meeting activities or designs that they will then take onto the campus and implement. This training sets the stage for the entire planning process, which relies on PTF members to do much of the work. The role of the consultant is to build capacity, teach and train, and guide the institution through the process. The consultant does not drive the process—the task force members do.

Although intense, the two-day training session will generate enthusiasm and momentum going forward. In addition, the task force members will actually experience several collaborative meeting designs that they will later use during Phase II (Data Gathering and Engagement). These are not simulations but rather real designs used to generate strategic information for the planning process. This firsthand experience enables them to better understand each design's strengths and flaws and potential applications.

Once trained, the PTF is expected to implement the same designs throughout the campus and community. This approach has several benefits. It:

- Builds the internal capacity of each task force member to engage in collaborative work. Faculty often report that these collaborative practices have influenced how they teach, while administrators say their meetings become dramatically different and more effective.

- Enhances the credibility of the planning process because insiders, not outsiders, are conducting the process. Stakeholders' level of trust in the planning process grows when they see one of their own facilitating meetings, engaging others, and creating transparency. People can clearly see how their voices and ideas inform the process.
- Creates ownership of the planning process because PTF members work hard to design a process that meets the unique needs and culture of their institution. The process is theirs, not something crafted by outside consultants and imposed upon the institution. During the training session, for instance, the PTF creates a communication plan, a work plan, and strategic database in a relatively short period of time. Members quickly learn that they can create a rigorous planning process without getting bogged down with details.

Although each PTF will bring its own character and complexity to the training session, several activities should occur in a natural order. The sample agenda below, for example, provides a good sense of how the two-day session would unfold, beginning each day at 8:30 a.m., and concluding each day at 5:30 p.m.

Because the meetings build on one another conceptually to create a holistic database, follow the sequence suggested below. Do not mix and match activities, unless you're using these collaborative designs for isolated purposes, such as a curriculum review or problem solving.

The general timeframes provide an idea of how long each training session and meeting design will take. Be sure to factor in several breaks as well as a lunch time, all of which should be determined by the co-chairs of the planning task force and any consultants.

SAMPLE AGENDA: 2-DAY TRAINING SESSION FOR THE PLANNING TASK FORCE

DAY ONE

Welcome and Introductions by the President   1 Hour

This will be the first opportunity for all PTF members to meet one another and introduce themselves. At a minimum, ask members to state their name, their role in the institution, how long they have worked on the campus, and one hope or aspiration they have for the institution.

The president should clearly communicate his or her deep appreciation for the PTF members' participation in the planning process, emphasizing the importance of their work for the future of the institution.

The Five-Phase Model   1 Hour

After outlining CSP's five-phase model, the consultants or co-chairs answer participants' questions. The goal is to give PTF members a sense of the journey they will be taking and what is expected of them along the way.

Accomplishments Design   1 Hour

PTF members identify past successes and distill the lessons learned that they can apply to the upcoming planning process.

Carousel Design   1 Hour

The PTF conducts a SWOT Analysis (Strengths, Weaknesses, Opportunities, Threats) for the institution.

Interview Design   **2½ Hours**

PTF members ask one another a set of strategic questions that will inform the planning process and create real data.

Day Two

Opening Remarks   **15–20 Minutes**

The facilitators recap the previous day's work, answer any questions raised by PTF members, and set the stage for the day's activities.

Future Timeline Design   **1 Hour**

Participants identify the events, trends, and issues that could impact the institution over the next five to 10 years.

Communication Plan   **1 Hour**

The task force identifies the key stakeholders who need to be engaged with and communicated to during the process. They also prioritize the stakeholder groups.

Cascading Agreement Design   **1 Hour**

Task force members create working agreements, or ground rules, to guide their work. The resulting agreements will enable them to work effectively and efficiently.

Talent Bank   **30 Minutes**

The group identifies people on campus, but not on the PTF, who might provide assistance during the planning process, such as facilitators, researchers, writers, and editors.

Engagement Work Plan   **30 Minutes**

The task force identifies which stakeholder groups it will communicate with and engage throughout the planning process. It also identifies who will work with each stakeholder group.

Question-and-Answer Session   **1 Hour**

This open-ended discussion gives everyone the opportunity to clarify expectations, review agreements, identify responsibilities, and ask nuts-and-bolts questions about the planning process.

Closing Remarks   **15–20 Minutes**

Ideally, the president will have attended the entire training session. In any case, he or she should extend thanks to the task force for the hard work that has already taken place and for what will follow and re-emphasize that the members' efforts will shape the institution's future.

The following pages provide greater detail on each meeting design used during the two-day training session. Using the example of Incredible University, we'll walk through each step of the designs so you can understand the flow of the training session and be able to effectively implement each design within your own institution. Remember, you can use these collaborative designs independently, for different purposes, or in the sequence that follows for planning purposes.

DAY ONE

Welcome and Introductions by the President

The president should open the session and, if possible, demonstrate a personal commitment to collaborative planning by participating in the entire two-day training. If scheduling conflicts or other obligations prevent the president from attending both days of the training he or she, at a minimum, should open and close the two-day session.

If the president is unable to attend the session's opening and closing, revisit the feasibility of implementing CSP at your institution. If the president cannot find the time to engage in the process, do not begin it. Do something else.

Here is a suggested process to follow for this portion of the session.

— After welcoming the PTF members, the president thanks them for their support and participation. The remainder of the president's brief remarks should:

- Emphasize how important the planning process is to the future of the institution
- Acknowledge that collaborative planning will require a lot of hard work and thinking over the next nine to 12 months
- Express the president's deep appreciation for the time and effort the task force will invest in the planning process
- Confirm that the institution will provide the support the task force needs to do its job (such as meeting space, technology, and the president's attendance at key meetings)

Facilitator's Directions

— Ask participants to introduce themselves by name, role in the institution, and years on campus.

— After participants have a sense of who else is in the room, ask: "What hope or aspiration do you have for Incredible University?" Then have each PTF member talk with the next person for about two minutes so both can share their hopes or aspirations. This pair-and-share design will be the first one all PTF members experience.

— Next, ask attendees to share their hopes and aspirations with the entire group. Capture all the comments on a flipchart so everyone can get a sense of what their colleagues envision for the institution. This exercise provides the first database of the entire planning process and helps set the tone for everything to come.

Compile these hopes and aspirations into one document and distribute a printed copy to all PTF members before the training session concludes and an electronic copy immediately afterward. Refer to this database periodically during the planning process. It can act as a touchstone for PTF members, especially during Phase III (Making Sense of the Issues), and serve as a framework for looking at all the data collected.

— Review the five phases of the collaborative strategic planning process, providing just enough detail for PTF members to feel comfortable with—but not overwhelmed by—the process. The goal is to provide a broad overview of the planning journey the members will be taking over the next nine to 12 months. Also explain that PTF members will be experientially taught several collaborative planning designs and be expected to use them.

Every member of the PTF should receive a copy of the executive summary that outlines the process (see Appendix B). Also post the executive summary on the planning Web site for campus stakeholders so there's no mystery surrounding the planning process.

FACILITATOR'S TIP

Do not confuse interactive, participative designs with energizers—exercises aimed at injecting energy and enthusiasm into a group, often in inauthentic ways. Energizers usually don't work well in higher education because academia resents being manipulated. If you decide to use an energizer, be aware that it could create a rough beginning for the planning process.

The Accomplishments Design
Level of Difficulty: Easy
Estimated Time: 1 Hour

The Accomplishments design is easy to facilitate, doesn't take much time, and builds a constructive database at the start of the planning process. In a short period of time, participants become more knowledgeable about the institution.

This design acknowledges that success, as well as failure, leaves clues. Every campus has many successes but, too often, they are not acknowledged or reflected upon. With this design, PTF members and other stakeholders have the opportunity to identify institutional successes and, more important, learn from them.

Logistics

Materials: Flipchart paper, 10 to 15 easels, tape, and markers

Space needs: Large, comfortable room with a lot of wall space

Number of participants: 10 to 50 (If you use this with 100 participants, you'll need a very large room, an enormous amount of wall space, and two facilitators)

Using 40 participants as the example, tape approximately 50 flipchart sheets to the room's walls. (Count on one sheet per person, plus a few extras in case participants need them.) Space the sheets generously apart to give people plenty of room to work.

Each sheet should look like this:

ACCOMPLISHMENT

1. What made it work, specifically?

2. What lessons do we need to bring forward as we plan for the future?

The room should look like this:

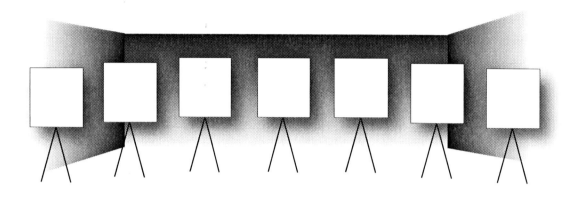

Facilitator's Directions

— Ask the participants to form 10 mixed groups of four participants. You can either have them organize themselves or use a counting-off method from one to ten.

— Say to participants, "Please think about the many accomplishments this university has experienced over the last five years. These accomplishments could be campus-wide or in your specific division, college, or office." For example:

- We successfully completed the business school accreditation process
- We have improved technology in every classroom
- Our campus communication system is very effective
- Our one-stop shopping for student registration has been a success
- We won our conference in lacrosse
- The debate team went to the national conference

— Ask each group of four to reflect on the past accomplishments of the university, capture the accomplishments on a flip chart, and answer the focus questions on the sheet (one accomplishment per sheet). The accomplishments don't have to be big or well-known; small successes are equally important (such as an improved office process, a co-curriculum course offering, or a decline in a particular dormitory's discipline referrals).

— Encourage participants to be specific when filling out the sheets; the more specific they are, the more valuable the information will be. Avoid global themes such as "good team work" and "we worked hard."

— Walk participants through an example before they begin the experience. For example:

Accomplishment: We have created an effective campus-wide communication process

What made it work, specifically?

- We did a campus-wide survey on communication vehicle preferences
- We appointed a "communication czar" at the VP level to raise the level of awareness and authority for the project
- We visited several other campuses that are known for effective communication systems as part of our research
- Louis and William were excellent co-chairs for the communication task force
- We listened to our stakeholders when they said they wanted a variety of communication vehicles (e.g., electronic newsletters, president's weekly note to campus, monthly town hall meetings)

Lessons to bring forward as we plan for the future

- Leadership matters so choose wisely
- Do your homework, don't jump to solutions
- Listen to stakeholders, it improves the outcomes

— To avoid redundancy, encourage participants to pay attention to what other groups are creating on their flipcharts. If a group finds it has an accomplishment also noted by another group, the two groups can briefly share their ideas and jointly describe the accomplishment.

— Give participants about 20 minutes to fill in the sheets. Make sure they stay in their groups of four while doing this.

> **FACILITATOR'S TIP**
>
> Give a half-time warning (10 minutes) to keep people on task and a two-minute warning toward the end of the Accomplishments design. Also ensure that people don't generate redundant information or become caught up in debating an accomplishment.

— After participants have filled in the Accomplishment sheets, ask each group of four to devote 15 to 20 minutes to two actions. First, the group should review all of the Accomplishment sheets in the room, take notes, and reflect on what they are learning. Second, each group's members should generally agree on the top three "lessons learned" from the entire database. Suggest that the criteria for the top three lessons meet the following standard: "What important lessons are critical to remember as we plan for the future of this institution? If we forget these lessons, we might fail in our endeavors."

— At the end of the allotted time for reviewing and distilling the essential lessons, ask each group to provide one lesson. In a round robin, take one idea from each group, making as many rounds as necessary to capture all the ideas. Record these lessons on a flipchart in full view of everyone, checking off similar ideas to start identifying the top priority lessons.

Here's an example of a master list of lessons:

1. Open, transparent communication throughout this planning process is essential. Stakeholders should have access to the relevant information they need. √√√√√√

2. No-baloney approach to everything. Share our victories as well as our mistakes. Be honest. √√√√

3. Without real faculty engagement in this planning process, it will fail. We saw that faculty involvement in the technology plan made all the difference in the world. √√√√

4. We need a way to keep score on progress and communicate this to campus stakeholders.

5. The president's visible involvement in the planning will be essential. √√√

6. We have to build on our many successes but we tend to focus on our weaknesses. √√

7. People will commit to hard work if they understand how it helps move the institution forward. √√√√√

At the end of a relatively short period of time, participants will have worked together to create a positive and strategic database that will inform the planning process. In addition, they will have experienced a low-risk, interesting, collaborative meeting design and seen how a large group of people can work in about an hour to create helpful information.

Schedule

Facilitator explains purpose of meeting and gives instructions	10 minutes
Facilitator counts off the groups	5 minutes
Small groups of three or four work together to fill in the flipchart sheets and create the database	20 minutes
Small groups look at all the sheets in the room to understand all the accomplishments and lessons and generally agree on the top three	10–15 minutes
Facilitator creates the master list	15 minutes
TOTAL	Approximately 1 hour

Note: A variation of this design, called Potholes, follows the same process but asks participants to identify the failures or missed opportunities rather than the successes. Taking the Potholes approach, however, requires a high level of trust within the group and openness to feedback. If you have no evidence of these qualities, do not use this design for identifying lessons from failures; the experience will be more polarizing than constructive. Using both the Accomplishments and Potholes designs, to identify lessons learned from successes as well as failures, provides a holistic database to inform the task force's thinking.

The Carousel Design
Level of Difficulty: Easy
Estimated Time: 45 to 50 Minutes

This highly interactive collaborative meeting design can be used effectively to gather information about significant topics (such as campus climate, ways to enhance institutional communication, and how to generate ideas for improvement). Its greatest value is its transparency: All ideas are shared openly, and no one can control the outcome.

Here's how you would use the Carousel to conduct a SWOT (Strengths, Weaknesses, Opportunities, Threats) analysis for Incredible University.

Logistics

Materials: Flipcharts, easels, a magic marker for every participant, masking tape, timer, and chimes (or a bell)

Space needs: Large, comfortable room where participants can move around easily, plus a lot of useable wall space

Number of participants: 10 to 40

Using 40 participants as the example, create four mixed groups of participants by having people count off from one to four. This will produce four groups of 10 people each. Clearly label and number the four focus questions on four different flipcharts posted around the room.

Your room should look like this:

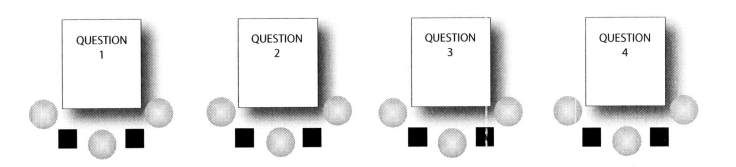

For a large group of 40, have several flipcharts at each station so people do not have to wait for others to finish writing their ideas. You can also tape extra flipchart paper on the walls near each station to enable several people to write simultaneously.

Facilitator's Directions

— Ask participants to go to the station that represents the number they were assigned (for example, 1, 2, 3, or 4).

— Instruct each group to read the focus question at their assigned station and *individually* record their responses directly on the flip chart. Make sure every participant has a magic marker. Say, "This is *not* about group agreement. We want individual responses. If you agree with another person's ideas, indicate your agreement by checking (√) the idea."

— Give each group about five minutes to read the focus question and individually record responses. Discourage people from talking or debating an idea on the flipchart. Encourage individual responses.

— At the end of the allotted time, use a bell or chimes to signal that it's time for each group to move clockwise to the next station. Make sure everyone stays with their group while the rotation occurs.

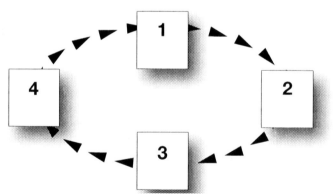

— Ask participants to read the previous group's input, individually check off the ideas with which they agree, and add their own ideas to the list.

— Continue the rotation until all four groups have visited all four stations and individually recorded their responses.

— Have each group return to its original question. A lot of new information will have been added to their original responses. Give them several minutes to read the new information and check off the answers with which they agree. Do not, however, have each group complete another rotation around the room to review all answers to all four focus questions. This will drain participants' energy and lead to information overload.

— Ask each original group to report the top four or five answers to their focus question. These will be easily recognized by the check marks. Limit the reports to one or two minutes.

— Tell participants that all the information created will be captured in electronic form and sent to them.

The PTF's SWOT Analysis for Incredible University might look like this:

STRENGTHS
High quality faculty √√√ √√√√ √√√
A great regional reputation √√√√ √√√√ √√
High-functioning cabinet √√√
We love the students √√√√ √√√√ √√√√
Great facilities √√√√ √
Academic excellence √√√√ √√√√ √
Commitment to access √√√√ √√√
Commitment to lifelong learning √√√√ √√√
High-caliber board √√√√ √

WEAKNESSES
Student life on weekends is boring √√√√√ √√√ √√
Enrollment is weak in the College of Allied Health √√√√ √√√
Technology is becoming outdated √√√√ √√√√
Lack of diversity in faculty √√√√ √√
Our endowment is too small √√√√ √
Our reputation is only regional √√√√
Transfer students don't make it here √√√√ √

OPPORTUNITIES
Local and regional businesses need job training in areas we excel √√√√ √√√√ √
Partner with an online, for-profit education company to put many of our
    courses online √√√√
Use our MBA students to create a massive marketing program for Incredible √√√
Rate of career changes in a lifetime are increasing, people will need more education √√√√
Adult student population is increasing dramatically √√√√

THREATS
Byrne University has begun a nursing program that will compete with ours √√√√ √√
Deferred maintenance is a growing problem and we don't seem to have a plan √√√√ √√√
State expenditures for higher education are being reduced √√√
Fundraising is expensive and very competitive √√√
Technological security on campus √√√√ √√
Changes in technology will increase obsolescence and cost
Number of regional high school students is declining √√√√ √√

Schedule

Facilitator welcomes participants, shares purpose, and gives directions for activity	5 minutes
Facilitator uses a counting-off method to create randomly mixed groups	5 minutes
The four groups answer the focus questions and rotate to all stations	20 minutes
Groups return to their original question, read the information, and check ideas with which they agree	5 minutes
Small groups select the top four or five ideas/answers for their focus question and prepare a brief presentation	5 minutes
Each small group gives a short presentation about its top four or five answers	5–10 minutes
Facilitator thanks participants and explains how the information will be used	2–3 minutes
TOTAL	Approximately 45–50 minutes

The Interview Design
Level of Difficulty: Moderate to Challenging
Estimated Time: 2½ Hours

This meeting design can change the way people think about collaborative planning because it is interactive, focused, interesting, and outcome-based all at the same time. It opens them to new possibilities and creative approaches to organizing and designing future meetings.

This type of design will show the PTF members how they can collectively engage large numbers of people in thinking about and planning for the future of their campus. It will enable the PTF to engage as many stakeholders as desired, creating a stakeholder database based on input from hundreds, if not thousands, of people.

You can use the Interview design with large groups of 50, 75, or even 100 participants. It may, however, present a logistical challenge because it calls for a large room so participants can move around quite a bit.

Logistics

Materials: 10 flipcharts, markers, note pads, pens, moveable chairs

Space needs: Very large, comfortable room with a lot of wall space

Number of participants: 10 to 100 (If you use this design with groups of 200 or more, you will need at least two facilitators)

Using 50 participants as the example, arrange the room in pairs of rows facing one another. If you have extra people (such as 52 instead of 50), place them on the end of one of the Row As. Assuming you have five planning questions, the room should look like this:

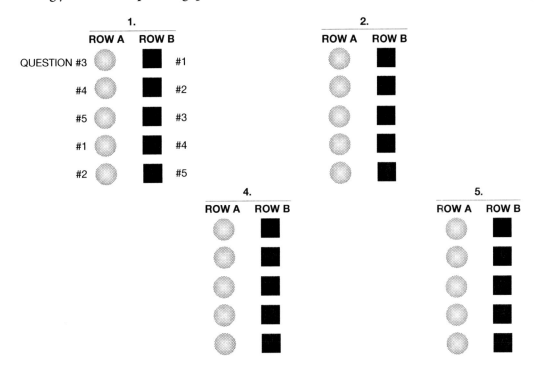

Here are some examples of strategic questions often asked on campuses:

1. What is the main reason we are not a stellar institution?

2. What makes you the most proud about this university?

3. How can we further improve campus-wide communication?

4. What challenges do you anticipate us needing to deal with effectively over the next five years?

5. What one piece of advice would you like to give to the president? To the trustees?

6. What institutional values must we preserve at all costs?

7. What can we do to improve diversity on this campus?

8. What best practice do you know about that would help us improve as an institution?

9. What key issues must we deal with if we are to achieve excellence as an institution?

10. What one thing must we change (for example, do more of, do less of, or get rid of) to succeed in the next one to three years?

11. How would you describe campus culture?

12. What do you enjoy about student life on campus? What don't you enjoy about student life?

13. What about our history helps us as an institution? Hinders us? Hurts us?

14. What institutional values inform and govern our behavior?

The PTF should determine the kinds of engaging, strategic questions they want to ask campus stakeholders to inform their thinking. We'll use these five focus questions to show how the design works.

- If you were talking with a colleague about Incredible University, how would you describe this place?
- What must senior leadership (the president and cabinet) do to ensure the success of the strategic planning process?
- What guiding principles should apply to this strategic planning process?
- What are some important questions we need to ask campus stakeholders about the institution?
- As PTF members, what concerns do you have about the collaborative planning process?

Facilitator's Directions

— Explain that the participants in Row A will start the interview process. They will ask their partner—the person sitting across from them—their focus question and record the unedited responses, for two minutes. Be sure to emphasize that the responses should not be edited; you don't want participants deciding on their own whether to include a partner's responses.

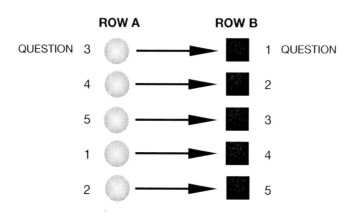

— For the next two minutes, switch the process: The participants in Row B ask the partners in Row A their focus question and record the unedited responses. Remember to stagger the questions in Row B so that participants do not ask the same question of one another.

— After Rows A & B have asked their questions and recorded the unedited responses, announce the next round. Ask people in Row B to move down one seat; the person at the end of Row B moves to the head of the row. Remind people in Row B to bring their question along when they move.

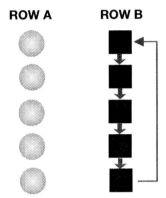

— Repeat the previous steps: People in Row A ask their question and record the responses, then Row B does its questioning.

— Continue the rotation until all the questions have been asked and answered. At the end of approximately 30 minutes, every person will have been interviewed five times, and they will have interviewed five people.

— After the initial interviewing process, have participants sit quietly for 10 to 15 minutes and organize their interview data into these three categories:

Facts: The responses or answers expressed by almost every person interviewed, which literally leap off the page. (It's fine if participants don't identify any facts.)

Trends: Responses given by two or three people. These are not as strong as facts.

Unique Ideas: Individual ideas that represent a different, creative, unique perspective or idea. It is not a laundry list of every other idea. Each person must judge if his or her interview data contain a unique idea to include in the database. (Again, it's fine if participants don't identify any unique ideas.)

— After individuals have organized their interview data into the three categories, they will be well-prepared for the discussion that follows. Ask them to join others with the same question. In the example with 50 participants and five questions, you would have five stations with 10 participants at each station.

The room should look like this:

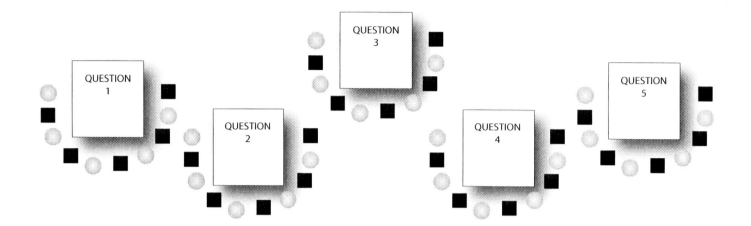

— Instruct the participants to use self-managed roles of facilitator, recorder, timekeeper, and presenter (see Appendix A). Give them 45 to 60 minutes to pool their group information. They should record the facts, trends, and unique ideas for their focus question on flipchart paper.

— After the five focus question groups have created the facts, trends, and unique ideas for their question, have each group present its findings to the larger group. Each presentation should take about three minutes.

— After the presentations, lead a brief discussion about participants' reactions to the shared information. Limit this discussion to 20 minutes.

— Remind participants that you will share the information in an electronic format as soon as possible.

FACILITATOR'S TIP

With the Interview design, pay attention to how each group is working together to make sure participants don't get bogged down in details or debate. Tell them to stay true to the data and capture the information in the three categories. Also, make sure the groups begin writing on the flipcharts about halfway through the time allotted. This ensures one group will not wait until the end of the allotted time to start writing and then keep the other groups waiting.

Here are two examples of responses to PTF focus questions:

What must senior leadership (the president and cabinet) do to ensure the success of the strategic planning process?

FACTS
√ They must be visible and engaged throughout the process
√ They must listen to people
√ They must share all the information we gather with campus stakeholders
√ They must be committed to implementing the strategic planning process outcomes

TRENDS
√ Have regular campus breakfast meetings to keep people informed about the process
√ The president should include updates about the planning process in his weekly letter to the campus
√ Let us know how the planning decisions will be made
√ Be transparent with the budget

UNIQUE IDEAS
√ Ask the mayor to participate in the planning task force
√ Identify faculty who have expertise in strategic planning and use them as a reality check throughout the process

What are some important questions we need to ask our campus stakeholders about the institution?

FACTS
√ What are the strengths of Incredible University? (What do you feel most proud about?)
√ What are some challenges facing this university over the next five to 10 years?
√ What two changes/improvements would you make with the physical plant/infrastructure of the campus?
√ What are the most important trends and issues we need to pay attention to as we plan for the future?
√ How would you describe the culture of Incredible University (for example, open, welcoming, critical)?
√ How can we improve the quality of student life on campus?
√ How would you describe the quality of our faculty's teaching in the classroom?
√ What institutional values should we truly live?

TRENDS
√ What are some areas we need to improve as an institution? (Please be specific.)
√ What is one piece of advice you would like to give to the president that would enable her to lead even more effectively?
√ What keeps us from being great at everything we do?
√ When you talk about Incredible University to your family and friends, what do you say?
√ How can we use technology to improve the educational experience in the classroom? Elsewhere?
√ How can we further improve campus communication?

UNIQUE IDEAS
√ What difficult issue do we need to openly discuss that currently is avoided?
√ How can we further improve collaboration across campus?

Schedule

The facilitator welcomes participants, explains the purposes of the meeting, and walks through the directions	10–15 minutes
Participants interview one another about the assigned questions	30–40 minutes
Participants individually organize their interview data into facts, needs, and unique ideas	15 minutes
Groups work with like questions, pool their information, and create presentations about their interview data	45–60 minutes
Groups report their findings	10–15 minutes
Facilitator conducts a brief discussion about responses to the overall data	15–20 minutes
TOTAL	Approximately 2½ hours

(Source: Rod Napier, president of the Napier Group, is the original thinker behind the Interview Design)

DAY TWO

The Future Timeline Design
Level of Difficulty: Easy to Moderate
Estimated Time: 1 to 1¼ hours

This meeting design enables groups both small (10 people) and large (100+ people) to anticipate the future events, trends, and issues that could potentially impact or influence the institution over the next five to 10 years. It is a highly interactive, interesting, and informative design that encourages people to look outward at external realities and create possible future scenarios. Its primary goal is to create a powerful database for strategic planning.

Logistics

Materials: Post-its, flipchart paper, magic markers, and masking tape

Space needs: Large, comfortable room with useable wall space (50 feet per timeline)

Using 48 participants as an example, tape 10 sheets of flipchart paper to the wall—one sheet per year for the next 10 years. (If participants number 100 or more, use two Future Timelines and two facilitators.)

The room should look like this:

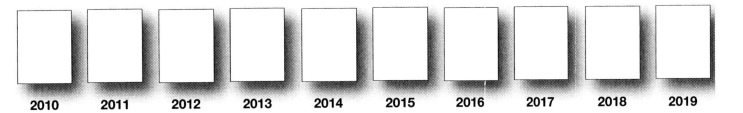

2010   2011   2012   2013   2014   2015   2016   2017   2018   2019

Facilitator's Directions

— Give each participant 10 Post-it notes.

— Instruct participants as follows: "Please think about the future events, issues, and trends that could impact or influence—either positively or negatively—the way Incredible University provides its services, conducts its business, or operates over the next 10 years."

— Provide several definitions on a flipchart or a handout. For example:

An event is a single occurrence. (Examples: passage of a piece of legislation, retirement of a president or chancellor, election of a new mayor or governor)

An issue is an important theme with substantial power and influence to impact an institution. (Examples: faculty compensation, student access, equity, use of adjunct faculty, technology in the classroom)

A trend is an ongoing set of circumstances that has consistency and momentum. (Examples: student demographics, aging faculty, increased competition from nonprofits, slowing down of the regional economy)

— After reviewing the definitions and checking for understanding, provide the following instructions:
- Please write down one event, trend, or issue per Post-it.
- Please indicate if a trend or issue will last for a while.
- Because we will review the Post-its in a few minutes, legibility is important.
- When you are ready, please go to the Future Timeline and populate it by placing your events, trends, and issues in the years you believe they will occur.
- If you see a Post-it on the Timeline that is similar to yours, please check (√) it to indicate agreement and discard your Post-it. This reduces redundancies and keeps the Timeline from becoming too cluttered.

— Give participants about 10–12 minutes to think, write on the Post-its, and populate the Future Timeline. This generates a tremendous amount of information for participants to distill and understand.

— Ask participants to create small, mixed groups of four. Participants can self-organize or use a counting-off method of one to 12, to produce 12 groups of four participants each.

— Instruct the participants as follows: "Please work with your group of four and review the Post-its on the timeline. Your goal in the next 20 minutes is to search through all the information and generally agree on the three most important issues, events, or trends—not three per category but three in total—that Incredible University must manage effectively if it is to thrive in the future."

— After the small groups have reviewed the Future Timeline and agreed on their top three issues, events, and trends, create a master list on flipchart paper in full view of everyone. Using the round-robin approach, take one idea from each group until all the ideas are captured. Check off similar ideas to begin prioritizing the list.

Typically, your master list will contain between 10 and 15 prioritized themes. Your list might look like this:

1. There will be a dramatic decrease in available students throughout the region √√√√
2. Technology costs will only increase due to the strong demand by students for cutting-edge technology √√√
3. Our dependence on state funding is erratic √√
4. Student housing needs great improvement √√√
5. Teaching in the classroom will be even more technology-based √√√√ √
6. Competition from nonprofits (e.g., University of Phoenix, Laureate) will greatly increase √√√√
7. Competition for top academic students will increase dramatically √√
8. Many of our current faculty will retire over the next decade √√√√ √√
9. Deferred maintenance will get very expensive √√√
10. Our president plans to retire in two years √√√√ √√

Schedule

Facilitator welcomes participants and explains the purpose and directions for the design	10 minutes
Participants think about the events, trends, and issues that could impact the institution; write them on Post-its, and populate the Future Timeline	10–12 minutes
Participants self-organize, or the facilitator uses a counting-off method, to place people into working groups of four participants	5 minutes
Small groups review the Future Timeline and generally agree on top three issues/events/trends	20 minutes
Facilitator creates prioritized master list using a round-robin approach	15 minutes
TOTAL:	Approximately 1–1¼ hours

Developing a Communication Plan
Level of Difficulty: Moderate
Estimated Time: 45 minutes

Careful attention needs to be paid to communicating to stakeholders in a variety of ways throughout the planning process. Poor communication can cripple a process and negatively impact campus climate and community.

Stakeholders will want information about what is going on, when meetings will be held, what themes are emerging from the engagement process, and so forth. If they don't receive timely, honest, and accurate information, they will feel devalued and marginalized. Then, they'll turn to the campus grapevine or rumor mill to get information.

The PTF can be proactive in creating and managing an effective, responsive, and agile communication system. To do so, PTF members must determine who needs to be informed, what key information needs to be communicated, and the most effective ways to communicate.

Using the Mindmapping tool to do a stakeholder analysis enables PTF members to clearly understand the different stakeholders who need to be engaged throughout the planning process. The Mindmap will provide a powerful, visual picture of the many stakeholders and helps prioritize the most important ones.

Logistics

Materials: Flipchart paper, easels, magic markers, Mindmapping instructions handout

Space needs: Large, comfortable room with moveable chairs and a lot of wall space

Number of participants: 10 to 40 (If your group numbers more than 50, have two recorders for the Mindmap.)

Using 30 participants for the example, tape several blank sheets of flipchart paper on a wall, creating a large expanse of paper approximately 5 or 6 feet tall and 7 or 8 feet wide. The room should look like this:

Facilitator's Directions

— Pass out copies of the Mindmapping technique instructions to all PTF members (see Appendix A).

— Take five to 10 minutes to review the Mindmapping technique to ensure everyone understands it.

— Ask PTF members to pick a partner and take about one minute to identify the relevant stakeholders who will need to be communicated with during the collaborative planning process. This "pair and share" will stir up ideas in a very short period of time.

— To create the Mindmap, ask PTF members to call out the stakeholder groups they have identified; record the information on flipchart sheets, in full view of everyone. Continue this process until members have shared all their possible stakeholders. At this stage, the list could easily number between 40 and 60 potential stakeholder groups with whom to communicate—far too many to meaningfully engage. The challenge becomes identifying the priority stakeholders—the 30 or 40 percent who need to be engaged face to face.

Your Mindmap might look like this:

— Use a multi-voting technique, such as Las Vegas Voting (see Appendix A). Give each PTF member five sticky dots; each dot represents a vote.

— Instruct PTF members to go to the large Mindmap and distribute their votes based on the key stakeholders they believe must be engaged in the planning process. For example, a PTF member may put two or three dots/votes on one key stakeholder group to communicate its high importance. They can put one dot per stakeholder group or put all five on one stakeholder group.

At the end of the voting, your Mindmap might look like the one below. As you can see, several key groups emerge as the priority stakeholders with whom to engage and communicate.

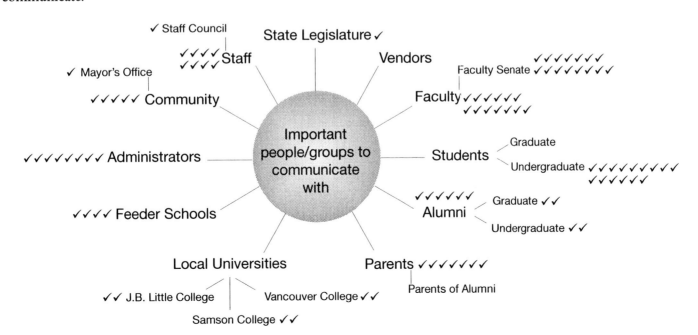

— Next, the group determines the most effective ways to communicate with each stakeholder group. Have a separate flipchart sheet labeled with each priority stakeholder group, and tape the sheets to the wall or on separate easels.

The room would look like this:

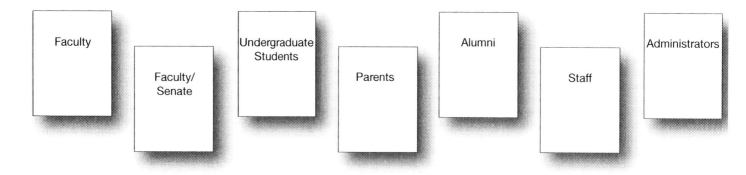

— Ask PTF members to move to the stakeholder groups about which they have knowledge or experience. Give them about 10 minutes to suggest ways, structures, and mechanisms to communicate with those stakeholder groups.

After the PTF members have provided their suggestions, the sheets on the wall might look like this:

FACULTY
President's weekly e-mail message
Breakfast meetings with key faculty
Weekly updates in campus newsletter
Voice mail updates
President's monthly lunch meeting

FACULTY SENATE
Make monthly presentations to faculty senate
Write a white paper about the planning process & distribute
Send a special bulletin to faculty senate

UNDERGRADUATE STUDENTS
Meet with student government
Meet with student's presidential council
Meet with campus ministry
Hold "chews and chats" at lunch time
Meet with student athletes' association
Have informal meetings in the student center

PARENTS
Communicate progress in quarterly parents' magazine
Meet with parents' association
Send out a special letter to parents
Have a large meeting with parents on parents' weekend

ALUMNI
Meet with alumni council
Hold several special evening meetings
Have a Saturday update at the football game (before the game)
Article in alumni magazine

STAFF
Meet with staff council
Meet with union officials
Send out a special newsletter
Include information in university newsletter
Have a monthly lunch meeting to update staff

ADMINISTRATORS
Update weekly with president's message
Have vice presidents hold a special meeting
Have special lunches with administrators
Include information in campus newsletter

This information helps set the stage for developing the work plan later in the training session. This activity gives PTF members the information they need to design a meaningful engagement process in the next phase of the planning process.

Schedule

Facilitator reviews the Mindmapping technique using a handout	5–10 minutes
Facilitator conducts the Mindmapping exercise	10–15 minutes
PTF members use Las Vegas Voting to determine key stakeholders	5–7 minutes
PTF members identify the best ways to engage and communicate with key stakeholders	10–15 minutes
TOTAL:	Approximately 30–45 minutes

Cascading Agreement
Level of Difficulty: Easy
Estimated Time: 1 Hour

This design, analyzed in Chapter 2, illustrates how a collaborative meeting design actually works. In addition to being an excellent teaching vehicle, the Cascading Agreement can be used to create working agreements or ground rules for a team, cabinet, or task force. (For example: We will not avoid difficult issues. We will not get caught in debate or diatribe. We will clarify our decision-making process before we make any group decisions.) It's also useful for dealing with significant institutional problems, such as campus morale or the freshman experience, or creating criteria for decision making about a difficult issue, such as budget cuts.

This design works easily with groups between 10 and 60, creating many opportunities for discussion and dialogue. This design has four steps: Create, Condense, Collaborate, and Communicate. The facilitator should let participants know that the meeting has several steps but *not* say what those steps are. If you describe the steps ahead of time, participants will out think the design and move to the end without the discussion necessary for a good outcome.

Logistics

Materials: Flipcharts, markers, paper, and pens

Space needs: Large, comfortable room with moveable chairs

This example shows how to use the Cascading Agreement design to generate guiding principles for the planning process. Participants should know up front that the goal of this design is to generally agree on three to five guiding principles.

Using 30 participants for the example, organize PTF members into sets of three with as much diversity as possible (for example, one faculty, one staff, and one student per group). One person in each small group should take responsibility for taking notes. The room should look like this:

Facilitator's Directions

— (The first step is to create.) Explain to participants that they'll be creating some principles to guide the collaborative strategic planning process. Note that, "These principles will help us—the planning task force—create the internal discipline we need to adhere to, hold ourselves accountable to the highest standards possible, and let all the external stakeholders know how this planning process will be conducted."

— Give the three-person groups 10 minutes to discuss five possible guiding principles for the planning process. Offer no more than two examples (so you don't do the thinking for the task force), such as "We want to be as inclusive as possible" or "We will be transparent with the information we collect."

— (The second step is to condense.) Ask the small groups to review their five guiding principles and reduce the list to the three best. Give participants five minutes to do this (if you give them much more, they will get caught in debate and detail.) Caution them not to clump all the ideas together when they reduce their list. For example: "We will have open and transparent communication while using a variety of communication vehicles" may be one sentence, but it contains two guiding principles.

— (The third step is to collaborate.) Ask each group of three to join with another group to form larger groups of six.

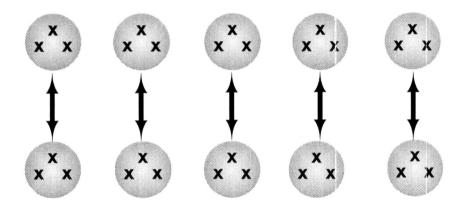

— Give participants 10 to 12 minutes to share each small group's three guiding principles and generally agree on the very best three that will be worthy of their commitment and set the standard for the institutional planning process. Provide another reminder about clumping principles; each principle should be specific and stand by itself.

— (The fourth step is to communicate.) Using the round-robin approach, take one (and only one) guiding principle from each group of six and create a master list, in full view of everyone. Make as many rounds as necessary to solicit all the guiding principles. The five groups of six (30 participants in total) can theoretically produce 15 guiding principles (three from each group), although you'll probably find a lot of common ground among the groups of six. If one group has a guiding principle similar to one offered by another group, they should indicate that fact so you can prioritize the list as you create it.

The group will probably generate a master list with eight to 10 potential guiding principles, which might look like this:

POSSIBLE GUIDING PRINCIPLES

1. We will strive to include as many stakeholders as we can in the input stage of the planning process
2. We are committed to timely and accurate communication to all stakeholders
3. We will create opportunities for feedback throughout the planning process
4. We are committed to using a variety of communication vehicles = high-touch and high-tech
5. We will address the tough issues and deal with them as best as we can
6. We will deal with problems and challenges as we encounter them (e.g., breakdown in communication, low morale in a division or department)
7. We will publish all our meeting minutes on the campus Web page for internal stakeholder viewing and feedback
8. We will clarify in advance how the PTF will make decisions
9. The president's involvement in CSP will be visible and meaningful
10. Throughout the planning process, we will include strategic information about the external environment

— Use the Las Vegas Voting design (see Appendix A) to winnow the list to a manageable size—between three and five principles that the task force can easily focus on. Give two dots/votes to every PTF member. Have participants place their dots on the guiding principles that will help make the strategic planning process successful and be worthy of their commitment.

After the Las Vegas Voting, your list might look like this:

POSSIBLE GUIDING PRINCIPLES

1. We will strive to include as many stakeholders as we can in the input stage of the planning process ✓✓✓✓ ✓✓✓✓ ✓✓✓✓ ✓

2. We are committed to timely and accurate communication to all stakeholders ✓✓✓✓ ✓✓✓✓

3. We will create opportunities for feedback throughout the planning process ✓✓✓✓

4. We are committed to using a variety of communication vehicles = high-touch and high-tech

5. We will address the tough issues and deal with them as best as we can ✓✓✓✓ ✓✓✓✓ ✓✓✓✓

6. We will deal with problems and challenges as we encounter them (e.g., breakdown in communication, low morale in a division or department) ✓✓

7. We will publish all our meeting minutes on the campus Web page for internal stakeholder viewing and feedback ✓✓✓✓

8. We will clarify in advance how the PTF will make decisions ✓✓✓✓

9. The president's involvement in CSP will be visible and meaningful ✓✓✓

10. Throughout the planning process, we will include strategic information about the external environment ✓✓✓✓ ✓✓✓✓ ✓

As you can see, principles 1, 2, 5, and 10 registered the highest votes.

Schedule

Facilitator shares purposes and outcomes of the design	5 minutes
Trios brainstorm ideas	10 minutes
Trios agree on their best ideas	5 minutes
Small groups of six work together and agree on the three best ideas	10–15 minutes
Facilitator records ideas from each group using a round-robin approach	10 minutes
Participants use Las Vegas Voting to identify the top four or five ideas/guiding principles	5 minutes
TOTAL:	About 1 hour

Creating a Talent Bank
Level of Difficulty: Easy
Estimated Time: 30 Minutes

Every campus has scores of talented people who, if asked, will lend their expertise and experience to the PTF. This meeting design helps identify these people and enroll them in the planning process. The content of this design also informs the next activity, the Work Plan.

Logistics

Materials: Flipchart paper, markers for everyone, masking tape, a bell or chimes

Space needs: A large, comfortable room and a lot of wall space

Number of participants: 10 to 50

Using 40 participants as the example, tape 8 to 10 flipchart sheets to the wall. Label the flipcharts to reflect the categories of people needed. Instead of the sheets being scattered around the room, it is best if all the flipchart sheets can all fit on one large wall.

The room should look like this:

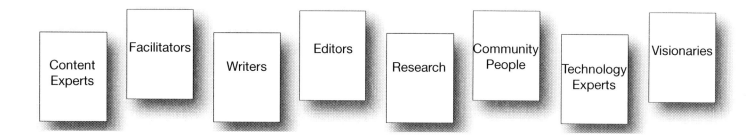

Facilitator's Directions

— Ask participants to pair up. Instruct the pairs of partners to talk with one another for two minutes to identify some of the talented people on campus who might help with the upcoming planning process. Some should be content experts who can help the task force think about important topics such as regional trends, technology, and demographics). Writers are another helpful category to have, as they can assist the task force in creating and editing concept papers (see Chapter 5).

Task force members should consider anyone who knows how to engage a group in meaningful discussion, whether that person works in the IT department (which may have experience conducting student focus groups) or in student life (which may provide training for student facilitators). As long as people outside the task force ask questions similar to those asked by PTF members (such as, "What are our strengths?" and "What challenges do you see going forward?"), the data generated will contribute to the planning process.

— Provide an example of the kind of information desired. For example:

Content Experts

- Dr. Jonsons in Sociology is a great resource about student demographics. Contact: Patrick Sweeney
- Steve Barnstein has written a book, *Future Trends in Technology*. Contact: Sara Johnston
- The Business School has excellent researchers in economic trends impacting the region. Don't know their names specifically, but we should talk to the dean. Contact: Barbara Ellis
- Professor Sandra Clark is recognized as expert in communication strategy—she might be helpful. Contact: Avik Roy

— After two minutes, ring a bell or chimes to end the conversations.

— Ask each group to go to the appropriate categories posted on the wall and fill in the person's name, some information about him or her, and whether either partner has a connection to the potential talent and could, for example, ask the person for help or invite the person to a meeting. When applicable, task force members should provide their own names for follow-up purposes. Allocate 15 to 20 minutes for participants to record the names and contact information, as shown in these samples of Talent Bank sheets.

FACILITATORS

- Jim Seitz in Student Affairs is an excellent facilitator (he is an assistant V.P.) (Paul Bryne)
- Dr. Johnson in the marketing/public relations department actually trains facilitators to do market research in his course (Bill Lentucci)
- The IT department has lots of good facilitators. They used them with the technology implementation this year
- Student Life has training for student facilitators, maybe we can use some of them?
- Most of the development people are very good facilitators (e.g. Mary, Joe, Pamela, Dr. Smith, William). We need to contact them (Patrick Hughes)

WRITERS

- Let's identify the faculty who teach freshman writing 101, they might be a good resource for us?
- Pamela Johnson is an excellent proposal writer, let's talk with her. Contact: Patrick Hughes, Bill Morer
- Ruth Haines in Business is a wonderful writer, she's published several books lately, very user-friendly writer. Contact: Caitlin Johnson
- Joan Reilly helped with our recent accreditation, as the lead writer. Contact: Mike DiBerardinis

— Capture the information regarding campus talent and distribute it to the task force members as soon as possible.

Schedule

Facilitator sets up the design and communicates what they are asking PTF members to do	5–10 minutes
PTF members work with a partner to identify potential talent	5 minutes
PTF members populate the talent bank with potential names and contact information	15–20 minutes
TOTAL:	30–40 minutes

Creating the Work Plan
Level of Difficulty: Easy to Moderate
Estimated Time: 45 minutes

At this stage, all PTF members will have experienced several collaborative designs, created useful information, and gotten a feel for each design's applicability. They are well-prepared to move forward and engage the campus stakeholders.

This culminating planning activity of the two-day training session builds upon the list of priority stakeholders identified during the Communication Plan design. That list provides the core elements of the PTF Work Plan, which will guide Phase II of the planning process (Data Gathering and Engagement). By generating the work plan, PTF members take ownership for the implementation of the engagement process over the ensuing two months.

Logistics

Materials: Flipchart paper, markers, masking tape

Space needs: Large, comfortable room with a lot of wall space

Using 40 participants as the example, tape two rows of 10 flipcharts to a wall in the room.

The room should look like this:

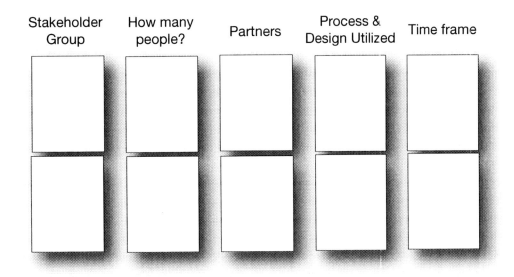

Stakeholder Group	How many people?	Partners	Process & Design Utilized	Time frame

Facilitator's Directions

— Give participants about five minutes to partner with a PTF member they don't have the chance to interact with regularly. Emphasize cross-boundary interaction by providing a flipchart with examples such as:

- Partners
- English professor with CFO
- Business school faculty with music faculty
- Development vice president with science faculty
- Athletic director with librarian
- Student life director with the director of physical plant

— After participants have paired off, give them five to 10 minutes to reflect on these two topics:

- The kind of stakeholder groups with whom they would like to engage during the next month or so
- The collaborative design(s) they would like to use for each stakeholder group they will work with. Although some stakeholders will be contacted and interviewed individually (such as the board of trustees and the local mayor), most people will be engaged through small and large group meetings.

FACILITATOR'S TIP

Remind PTF members that they can engage more than one group of stakeholders if they believe they have the time and energy to do so. Any members who work with two or more groups need to indicate this fact on each stakeholder group's work plan.

— Finally, give the groups 10 to 15 minutes to transfer their decisions (who they will engage and how) to the large work plan on the wall.

The wall might look like this:

Stakeholders	# People	Partners	Process/Design	Time Frame
Mayor's Office	10	Dr. Johnson & Pat M.	1:1 Interviews	2 weeks
Alumni Board	50	Raheem & Mary C.	Future Timeline	1 month
Parents Assn.	100	Dr. Tom Nicoletto & Bill L.	Interview Design	2 weeks
Student Government	20	V.P. D'Angelo & Peter	Carousel Design	1 week
Parallax Foundation	2	Co-chairs	1:1 Interview	2 weeks
High School Seniors	100	Peter Jonas, Joan, and Mary R.	Carousel Design	1 month
High School Principals	25	Monique & Lisa	Interview Design	1 month
Chamber of Commerce	35	Dr. Byrne, V.P.	Future Timeline	1 month
Board of Trustees	30	Marketing Co-chairs	Future Timeline	6 weeks

Schedule

Facilitator explains the design to PTF members	5 minutes
PTF members choose a partner to work with during the next phase of the process	5 minutes
PTF partners discuss what stakeholder groups they would like to engage and the possible designs to use	5–10 minutes
Partners come up to the Work Plan and sign up for the stakeholder groups they would like to engage	10–15 minutes
TOTAL:	30–40 minutes

Concluding the Training

Having worked hard during the two-day training session, PTF members will be tired but enthused about the different ways to gather data and engage campus stakeholders. They will also see that they have created a lot of strategic information, much of it new, for the planning process.

To end the final session on a positive note:

— Conduct a brief question-and-answer session to address any remaining questions.

NOTES TO PTF CO-CHAIRS

Here are some suggestions for preparing for the next phase of collaborative planning (Data Gathering and Engagement).

- Reiterate that the people who pair up for the Work Plan design will continue working together in pairs to facilitate and implement the collaborative designs they have all learned together. Working with a partner during the data-gathering phase helps model cross-boundary collaboration to stakeholders and simply provides another pair of hands and eyes to help facilitate a meeting. Although most of the collaborative designs don't require expert facilitation, they do have numerous logistical details; two people can better pay attention both to the stakeholder group they are working with and the details of conducting a meeting. Plus, the partners can serve as a resource to one another by offering advice, identifying challenges, and helping brainstorm ideas. If you haven't been formally trained to conduct a meeting for 50 people, it's good to have a friend in the room.

- After PTF members have migrated to those stakeholders groups with whom they believe they can be most effective, identify any important stakeholder groups that no one signed up to work with. Develop a plan to engage any groups missed in the initial round of creating the work plan.

- Electronically capture all the data from the work plan and send it to all PTF members as soon as possible. Also place the work plan on the PTF Web site.

- Communicate to PTF members that they need to implement their interactive stakeholder meetings within the next 30 days. Encourage them to begin as soon as possible; if the engagement process is delayed, you'll end up with many members trying to cram many stakeholder meetings into the last few days of Phase II.

- Don't over-think or over-plan Phase II. Although some people prefer Gantt charts and critical-path charts, fancy project management tools aren't necessary to keep tabs on the progress being made. You simply need a sense of which stakeholders have been engaged and when. PTF members can provide this information at the end of each stakeholder meeting, along with a transcription or summary of the data provided by the stakeholders. Post this information on the PTF Web site for all task force members to view.

- Consider identifying a data manager to manage all of the information flowing in from PTF members. Usually an administrative assistant or secretary can fulfill this important role, which includes updating the PTF Web site with the most recent information.

- About two or three weeks after the training, convene a PTF meeting to check in with members, share any lessons learned about stakeholder engagement, and continue building a sense of community. This "chew and chat" meeting should include some type of food and take about one hour.

— Ensure that PTF members understand that they are expected to engage their identified stakeholder groups as soon as possible (within 30 days), transfer data gathered from stakeholders to electronic form, inform the PTF co-chairs about their activities, and periodically check the PTF Web site to see what information other groups are generating.

As outlined above, the two-day training session covers a lot of territory in a relatively short period of time. Day One might go slowly because the people are unfamiliar with one another and with the collaborative meeting designs. Day Two tends to move faster because PTF members have developed a feel for the designs, produce strategic information, and have a good time. You will also see the beginning of community building without resorting to any team-building exercises or group energizers. When PTF members jointly focus on tasks that have value for the institution, they unconsciously build relational capital.

chapter 4

PHASE II—
DATA GATHERING
AND ENGAGEMENT

The data gathering and engagement (DG&E) phase sets collaborative strategic planning (CSP) apart from the data-driven, survey-focused, top-down approach that many institutions have traditionally favored.

The main purpose of the DG&E phase is to connect with stakeholders throughout the institution and engage their thinking and solicit their ideas. This is done primarily through the interactive and participative designs the PTF learned in its initial training session. The engagement process is intentionally low tech, using simple tools such as flipcharts and comfortable rooms with moveable chairs and plenty of useable wall space. Although technology has a role in this process, it does not drive it. Human interaction does.

The collaborative meeting designs will lead to several developments on campus:

- People will see the power of the highly engaging and outcome-based designs and become genuinely interested in—and enthusiastic about—the planning process.
- Stakeholders will become smarter about the institution because large numbers of people will share their ideas, perspectives, hopes, and aspirations. Using the Interview or Future Timeline design, for example, enables you to engage 50 or 100 people in thinking about the trends and strategic issues affecting the institution from a perspective more personal than you'd get with surveys.
- When stakeholders see their peers and colleagues doing the work of strategic planning, they better understand that the process must be important to the future of the institution because the best and brightest people are involved. Stakeholders also witness collaboration with partner pairs (such as pairing a physics professor with a vice president of development), which may not be typical within the institution's culture.
- Stakeholders will feel as if the planning process is not something done to them by outsiders (in other words, consultants) but something done *with* them by known and credible people.

CROSSING THE LINES

When one university surveyed faculty after the planning process concluded, it found that the cross-pair approach to data gathering registered the highest number of favorable impressions. Faculty noted that the collaborative planning process marked the first time English professors visited the physics department, the music school visited the business school, and the technology folks visited the athletic department.

- People on campus—particularly faculty—will want to use some of the collaborative meeting designs in their departments, divisions, and work units. (Have extra copies of the designs to give to interested participants.)

As the PTF members begin to engage the campus with their collaborative designs, many people will have questions about the process, make suggestions, and offer to help. Be prepared with a well-organized, informative, and user-friendly public Web site. If stakeholders find it difficult to obtain the information they seek, skepticism about the process will develop.

Stakeholders should know not only where to go for information but also who to contact if they have questions or advice. The PTF co-chairs are natural conduits for information sharing and answering stakeholder questions. That's why one of the co-chairs should attend each meeting with external stakeholders, such as community members or the chamber of commerce. Even the president may need to become involved in some meetings with external constituents, which often take time to organize.

NOTES TO PTF CO-CHAIRS

To help manage the data generated through the engagement process, establish protocols such as the following.

- Early in Phase II, communicate to the pairs of partners that they should organize the information they gather before submitting it to a central location. The last thing you want to receive is a bundle of flipchart paper that still needs to be deciphered and typed.

- Every two weeks, send reminders to any partner pairs who have not completed their assignment. To further prod them into action, ask if you can do anything to support their efforts. For example, make sure the partner pairs are ready and well-prepared for their interactive meetings, especially those with external stakeholders. (Internal stakeholders tend to be more forgiving if one of their own makes a mistake with a collaborative meeting design.)

- Have a system for assessing who is talking to whom throughout the DG&E phase. Share this information with all PTF members by providing a weekly snapshot of what's scheduled to happen when. This communication not only keeps people informed but also motivates the slowpokes. About 50 percent will start right away. Twenty-five percent will need a little proding and will start about half way through and 25 percent will wait until the last minute.

- When you receive a report from one of the interactive meetings, personally thank the PTF members who served as facilitators. Rather than a blast e-mail, take the personal approach—make a phone call, drop by someone's office, or send a personalized e-mail. A note from the president adds a special touch.

- During the DG&E phase, which can easily take two or more months, organize several brief get-togethers. Held every two or three weeks, these voluntary meetings will often draw as many as 85 percent of the task force members. If possible, build the meeting around a breakfast, lunch, or dinner to solidify the group's sense of community. At these working meals, PTF members can share what they are learning through their engagement with stakeholders.

Planning Updates (Chews & Chats)
Level of Difficulty: Easy
Estimated Time: 1 Hour

Although technology can provide information and has an important role in CSP, face-to-face interaction with stakeholders always takes preference. Use Planning Updates—an adaptation of the Axelrod Conference Model Walk-Thrus (1999)—when you want to

- Inform and update campus stakeholders about the collaborative strategic planning process, both its content and current phase
- Model transparency about the CSP
- Solicit ideas and feedback from participants about institutional issues
- Build a sense of community on campus

Ideally, schedule a planning update every two weeks, especially during Phases II and III of the planning process. The meetings will keep people informed, gather meaningful feedback, and improve communication and credibility.

If you set up the planning updates as "chews and chats" by including some type of food with the dialogue, you'll probably attract more stakeholders. Of course, you don't have to serve a four-course meal, just something simple such as coffee and donuts or pretzels and soft drinks. Involving food in the planning updates tends to support a feeling of community—when people share food, they will feel more connected to one another and more willing to work hard to accomplish meaningful goals.

Logistics

Materials: Flipchart, easels, informational handouts, feedback form, overhead projector

Space needs: Large, comfortable room

Number of participants: 10 to 50

Facilitator's Directions

— Welcome the participants, introduce the PTF co-chairs or members, and review the purpose of the meeting.

— Distribute handouts with pertinent information on the planning process; replicate the same information in a PowerPoint presentation that everyone can view simultaneously.

FACILITATOR'S TIP

Rather than stick to the same schedule all the time, hold planning updates in different locations around campus and at different times during the day—morning, lunch time, late afternoon, and even at night. At one research university, the PTF members resisted when someone suggested conducting a planning update at 7 p.m. Everyone thought stakeholders would be too busy to attend at that time, yet more than 200 people showed up for that evening meeting, which proved to be one of the most productive of the entire planning process.

Here is an example of what and how to communicate to the stakeholders who attend:

PLANNING UPDATE

In our strategic planning process, this is what we have discovered from the questionnaires we have collected. The 1,585 responses came from 725 undergraduates, 112 faculty members, 63 administrators, 442 alumni, and 243 parents.

The core values of the college ranked in priority order:

1. Our students (67%) believe that the student-teacher relationship is critical to student learning and our mission.
2. Having a close community feeling is important to a majority of our employees and students.
3. Academic excellence and integrity are core to what makes us distinctive. People are very proud of our academic reputation.
4. Our dedication to "service for others" is highly valued and must be preserved as a core element of our institutional mission.
5. Lifelong learning is a goal for many of our current students (61%) and valued highly by other stakeholders (44%).

Our stakeholders believe the following challenges, ranked in priority order, must be managed strategically over the next five years:

1. Maintaining and improving our academic excellence.
2. Building positive relationships with the surrounding community.
3. Our physical plant must be improved.
4. Improving communication throughout the college is essential for community building.
5. More parking for students, staff, and faculty must be available.
6. Security and safety on our campus need to be improved.

The critical current issues we need to manage are:

1. The growth of our undergraduate population is at an all-time high. We need to make important and wise decisions regarding growth.
2. Security and safety on our campus must be dealt with immediately.
3. Responding to the recent Middle States Evaluation is important, especially in the areas of faculty-administration relationships and diversity on campus.

— Take 15 to 20 minutes to review the information provided. To ensure everyone understands the information being presented, solicit questions and clarifications.

— Ask participants to "pair and share" with the person next to them. Give these pairs about five minutes to discuss their reactions to the information. To encourage dialogue, suggest that participants talk about:

- What they liked about the information
- What concerns they have
- What discoveries or learning they have experienced
- What questions they have about the presented material

— After the pairs have shared their thoughts, conduct a 20- to 30-minute open discussion regarding people's reactions. The purpose is to engage people, listen to what they have to say, and answer any questions they have.

— Have someone write down people's reactions and questions on flipchart paper, in full view of all participants. This creates a record of the conversations, provides structure, and emphasizes that all questions and ideas have value. Assure participants that any unanswered questions will be addressed via an established communication system (president's e-mail, campus voice mail, Web page, newsletter, other update meetings, and so forth).

— Distribute a short, anonymous survey—containing no more than five questions—to obtain feedback about participants' reactions to the shared information. You might ask, for example:

- Overall, how did you find this presentation? Choose from 1 (not useful), 2 (somewhat useful), 3 (good, solid information), 4 (very useful), 5 (outstanding)
- How can we further improve our communication with you?
- What questions do you still have about the planning process?
- What advice can you give us about improving our planning process?
- What are people saying about the planning process? What's the word on the street?

This snapshot of what people are thinking and feeling should be summarized and shared with participants as soon as possible. Reporting the findings—especially if they aren't all positive—takes courage, but it will enhance the credibility of the planning process.

Schedule

Welcome and introduction to the activity	5 minutes
Presenter reviews the important information	15 minutes
Participants engage in a "pair and share" to discuss their reactions	5 minutes
Presenter facilitates open discussion for all participants	30 minutes
Presenter asks participants to complete a short questionnaire	5 minutes
TOTAL:	1 hour

Surveys of Stakeholders

Most strategic planning efforts include an overabundance of surveys. Unfortunately, too many of these surveys are too long, don't ask the right questions, are more quantitative than qualitative (favoring numbers over ideas), and value efficiency over effectiveness.

Still, surveys have a place in strategic planning, especially if the president or PTF members want to conduct some. Do not, however, make a survey the primary source for information collected from stakeholders. There is nothing collaborative about surveys.

If you do use a survey, keep it short (between five and seven questions) and ask strategic questions such as:

- When you talk about this university to a friend or colleague, what do you say? How do you describe this institution?
- What three things would you change or improve about this institution? Why?
- What are some of the strengths of this institution? What do we do well?
- If you have one hope or aspiration for this university, what would it be?
- How can we further improve our academic excellence?
- What is one issue we need to tackle straight on in order to achieve excellence?
- What gets in the way of us achieving excellence in academics, athletics, student life?
- What is one piece of advice you would like to give to the president?
- How would you describe our institutional values?
- What future challenges do you think we as an institution will face?
- How would you describe communication in this university? Are you satisfied with the way communication works here?
- What advice can you give us that would make our strategic planning the best process possible?
- What do our competitors say about us? What is the word on the street? How do you know this?
- What do you think about our technological capacity? What are our strengths and weaknesses regarding technology?
- What issues and trends do you see as potentially affecting or influencing how this institution provides its services?

Choose questions that stimulate thinking and provide the task force with the best information possible. The best source of questions is the task force itself, whose members know the institution well.

Once drafted, the survey can be posted on the public planning Web site for people to complete online, if they wish. Most important, when you solicit answers from stakeholders, always report the results back to them.

The Values Discussion

CSP creates the opportunity for campus-wide discussion on institutional values—the qualities or characteristics that guide decision making, help the institution steer clear of problems, and align stakeholders toward a common good. This can be a delicate, volatile, exciting, and emotional discussion as stakeholders talk about what truly matters to them.

Just stating a set of values is not enough, as evidenced by the many corporations whose leaders espoused integrity, honesty, and honor yet ripped off stakeholders and stockholders at the same time. True values are lived behaviors—what an outsider would observe in the daily life of the institution while attending classes, going to meetings, and participating in celebrations, for example.

GETTING PERSONAL

One-to-one interviews offer another effective mechanism for obtaining data from stakeholders. Although time-intensive, personal interviews are recommended for interaction with key stakeholders such as the board chair, local mayor or legislator, and former president.

At one university, the president insisted that the PTF interview all trustees and high-level local businesspeople. Each PTF member interviewed three of these special stakeholders, most of whom expressed deep appreciation for the personal interaction. These stakeholders provided a deep, strategic database and often revealed their affection—and sometimes passion—for the institution. When the institution conducted its vision conference (see Chapter 6), most of the external businesspeople readily agreed to participate. Connections were built, relationships were made or remade, and the institution obtained excellent information.

How an institution lives its values is unique. As an example, many institutions list integrity as a value, yet each institution will take a distinctive and special approach to exhibiting that value. What excellence means for a top-tier research institution and what it means at a community college may be dramatically different but lived just as well.

Genuine institutional values are also enduring: They stand the test of time. They don't change much over time, especially not to fit the trends of the day. They can be interpreted differently over time as an institution grows and improves but tend to be sustained over decades.

Some campuses find themselves adrift because they lack institutional values or experience confusion about what their values mean. Led by its leaders, each campus needs to define institutional values in its own way, beginning with the data gathering phase of CSP.

The first discussion should start with the PTF, a group of highly credible people who represent important stakeholders and leaders in the institution. It is also a safe place to begin the dialogue because these individuals know the institution, care for it, and have built a sense of community. The president or co-chairs should convene a special meeting of the PTF to discuss institutional values. A trusted consultant, a former trustee, or a faculty member might facilitate this meeting so everyone on the PTF can fully participate.

The PTF values discussion should last approximately two hours to encourage dialogue. Remember and make adjustments for the Rule of Four (see Chapter 2) so all voices in the room have the opportunity to be heard. Techniques such as pairing and sharing can start the dialogue, or have small, mixed groups of three answer a focus question and then report their discoveries and discussions to the large group.

Many collaborative designs are fast-paced and have little built-in reflection time. They gather a lot of information and ideas but don't really facilitate deep discussion. Rather than employing a specific design for a values discussion, select several focus questions to stimulate interaction and dialogue. For example:

- When you think about our institutional values, how would you describe them to an outsider?
- Do you see instances where our stated institutional values don't match what we do?
- Can you tell a story that best exemplifies our institutional values?
- What institutional values do we need to have in the future?

Someone should record the essence of what was discussed—but not all of the details—and provide a summary for participants. You might need to hold several of these discussions with task force members before asking them to lead values discussions with their stakeholder groups (such as faculty, staff, administrators, business school). PTF members should also talk with the board of trustees (led by the president), alumni groups, and members of the local community.

A QUESTION OF VALUES

One university undertaking the planning process had the opportunity to purchase a local research hospital. The visionary president saw this acquisition as the last jewel in the crown that would propel the institution to the top tier of its class. Excitement was palpable; a sense of urgency and a hint of history making permeated the campus. Yet there was a problem.

Some PTF members discovered that the hospital engaged in limited research that ran counter to the institution's stated and religious values. Once this became evident, the fanfare and excitement waned immediately and all talk of an acquisition ceased. The president and stakeholders clearly understood they could not betray the institution's values.

Be sure to build time for values discussions into the schedule during Phases II and III, which give you a total of four to six months to conduct the dialogues. All values conversations should conclude before the strategic plan and a values statement are created for review throughout the campus.

chapter 5

PHASE III—
MAKING SENSE
OF THE ISSUES

Once members of the Planning Task Force (PTF) have held their meetings with various stakeholders and compiled the results, they need opportunities to process all the information gathered. Only by considering and sorting through the data can they see patterns emerging and eventually identify the dominant strategic themes.

This phase has two main components: a full-day Sensemaking Meeting and the creation of concept papers. It draws together the results of several months of stakeholder engagement and dialogue and sets the stage for Phase IV (Vision Conference).

The Sensemaking Meeting
Level of Difficulty: Moderate
Estimated Time: 1 Day

During this day-long meeting, task force members will

- Share what they have learned from their stakeholder meetings and interactions
- Begin to distill all the information generated
- Generally agree on the most important strategic themes for the planning process
- Organize themselves for the next steps in the planning process
- Agree on roles and responsibilities going forward

To maintain participants' interest and enthusiasm during the Sensemaking Meeting, schedule a break every 45 minutes. That gives people time to chat with others, think about other topics, and take care of any pressing business. Participants will return from each break fresher mentally and quite willing to learn what's next.

Logistics

Materials: Round tables, flipcharts, markers, 50 to 70 strips of paper (15 to 25 flipchart sheets cut into thirds)

SENSEMAKING MEETING SUGGESTED AGENDA

8:30 a.m. to 5 p.m.

- **Welcome PTF members.** Co-chairs—and the president, if possible—welcome the task force members and express thanks for the work completed to date.
- **Share stakeholder data.** Partners who worked together during the engagement process present what they learned from their meetings with stakeholders.
- **Discuss ideas with the entire task force.** After all the partners have made their stakeholder presentations, the entire PTF participates in a facilitated group discussion.
- **Identify strategic themes.** Small, diverse groups work together and agree on the essential themes to think about and plan for during the next phase of CSP.
- **Create a strategic planning model/map.** Task force members organize the potential planning themes into conceptual "buckets" (such as academic excellence, student experience, and research) to focus the information and ideas going forward.
- **Introduce the idea of concept papers.** The facilitator introduces a strategic planning tool for organizing the information in preparation for the vision conference.
- **Self-organize into concept groups.** PTF members select the concept they would like to work on, then agree on roles and a schedule for producing the concept paper.
- **Questions and Answers.** The PTF co-chairs outline the next steps and answer questions.

Facilitator's Directions

— Welcome participants, thank them for the hard work they have already completed, and outline the goals for the day.

— Ask the pairs of partners to share what they learned from their stakeholder engagements. Each brief presentation (between three and five minutes in length) should be supported by a one-page handout with highlights of their findings. A brief question-and-answer period, limited to three minutes, should follow each presentation so the partners can clarify any misunderstandings (but not debate the findings).

— To encourage PTF members to pay close attention to every presentation, distribute a listening guide with two or three questions for them to focus on. For example:
- What emerging themes are you noticing?
- What surprises or discoveries are you experiencing as you listen to your colleagues' presentations?
- What important and critical ideas do we need to pay attention to as we plan for the future of Incredible University?

FACILITATOR'S TIP

Stage the partners' presentations over time to avoid the meeting becoming a "data dump" where a few people drone on and everyone else loses interest after about 30 minutes. Say, for example, you have 22 presentations from PTF members because 22 different groups were solicited during the data gathering phase. Schedule seven presentations, each lasting about five minutes (including a brief Q&A), followed by a 10-minute break. After the break, have a second round of seven presentations (with Q&A) and another 10-minute break. Finish with the last round of eight presentations.

Another option is to hold a large group discussion following each break. Take three to five minutes to solicit answers to questions such as "What resonates with you at this time?" and "What ideas strike you as most important?" Write the responses on flipcharts, in full view of everyone, and refer to them after all the presentations have been given. (Remember, at this stage you are simply tracking the conversation, not debating or agreeing on anything.)

— Facilitate a large group discussion to engage the thinking of PTF members, begin making sense of all the information gathered, and gain some perspective on what people learned from the presentations. Schedule this discussion for at least 30 minutes but no more than 45 minutes; otherwise, the conversation will wander off course or become too detailed. Ask participants to

- Identify the consistent themes emerging from the presentations
- Discuss what they have learned from all the meetings
- Identify any surprises or discoveries they have experienced in the information presented

— Ask PTF members to self-organize into diverse groups of four (faculty, staff, administration). Emphasize that partners from the presentations should not work together.

— Once participants have formed the groups, give the following instructions: "Please take the next 15 minutes to discuss with your three colleagues the most important themes and ideas you have heard from the presentations. Use your listening guide questions as a framework for your discussions. We would like you to generally agree on the five or six most important themes we need to plan for as we think about the future of Incredible University. Please record your agreed-upon planning themes on the 1/3 flipchart sheets provided. Once you have completed the sheets, post them on the Planning Wall."

At this stage of the design, you could easily have 40 or 50 planning themes in random order.

Your Planning Wall may look something like this:

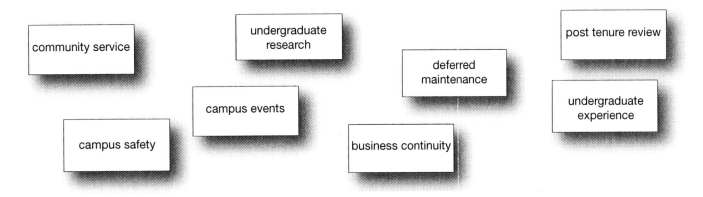

— Create three, large, mixed groups by having PTF members count off (from one to three). Provide the following instructions:

> "All PTF members with number one, please come up to the planning wall and begin to organize the different themes in a coherent manner. You can get rid of redundant ideas—you'll probably find many—and clump similar ideas. If a particular idea resides in more than one planning theme, record it on one of the blank strips of flipchart paper. You have four minutes to do this, and you *cannot talk* during the organizing process." (Note: If you allow the first group to talk, participants will get caught up in debate and talking about details that don't matter, which will bog down the process.)

— After four minutes have passed, ask the first group to sit down and invite all PTF members with number two to come up to the Planning Wall. Provide the following directions: "Continue to organize the themes into a coherent, conceptual model. *Do not talk* while you are doing this. You have four to five minutes."

— After the second group has refined the work begun by the first group, invite the third group to come up to the Planning Wall and do a final edit of the themes. Also instruct the third group to place headlines at the top of each planning theme category (such as student experience, academic excellence, and diversity). Here's what else is different: The third group can talk as its members do their work. Give them about five minutes to discuss, organize, and complete the planning themes.

The visual map creates the conceptual buckets that will focus the strategic planning efforts going forward. It may look like this:

STUDENT EXPERIENCE
community service
undergraduate experience
campus events
engaged student life

ACADEMIC EXCELLENCE
research
post tenure review

OPERATIONS
business continuity
campus safety
deferred maintenance

— Allocate about 45 minutes to present the notion of concept papers and the role these documents play in the strategic planning process. Emphasize these points:

- The conceptual buckets identified on the visual map will serve as themes for short concept papers. Each concept paper focuses on one strategic theme or area that the university needs to plan for in the future.

- Concept papers contain concrete information for use by both external and internal stakeholders. They are not intended to encourage "blue sky" thinking.

- PTF members will write the concept papers, which will be used during the up-coming vision conference (see Chapter 6) to educate and ground the participants in reality.

- PTF members do not need deep expertise in a particular area to volunteer for a concept paper. Each writing team has many different roles (writing, editing, research, and so forth), offering many ways to contribute.

- Each PTF member must serve on one writing team and play an active role in the concept paper's development. In this way, the PTF members will own the creation of the concept papers.

- Each concept paper will have a champion or chair to organize the efforts of the writing team and oversee the production of a quality product.

- Writing concept papers is not an onerous task. PTF members who have high expectations about the quality of the document—especially faculty—need to understand that they will be producing a short document (five pages, maximum) and not a footnoted thesis.

— Ask the PTF members to self-select the concept paper they would like to work on. Caution against having too many people work on one concept paper. For example, if you have 35 or 40 PTF members and seven strategic themes, 16 PTF members shouldn't sign up for the same theme.

— Before PTF members leave the meeting, thank them for their participation and acknowledge that more quality work still needs to be done. Also answer any questions so all members leave with a clear sense of what they need to do next and agreement on the time frames. Build 15 to 30 minutes into the agenda for this wrap-up session.

Writing a Concept Paper

The purpose of concept papers is to inform and educate readers who may have little knowledge or expertise about a particular subject. They should be written in user-friendly language that a layperson can easily understand and convey essential strategic information with little fluff. Each concept paper—ranging from three to five pages in length—should take no more than 15 minutes to read; in other words, it is not an academic tome.

In addition, concept papers

- Aim to manage the information overload that can easily occur in a planning process.

- Do not lobby for a particular viewpoint or attempt to sway the reader. They need to be neutral in tone, presenting the facts, not opinions, about a particular strategic theme.
- Should enable any reader to grasp the critical elements of a particular issue and understand the decisions that need to be made.

Here's an outline of the topics a concept paper on technology might include (see Appendix C and Appendix D for sample concept papers):

Background. Provide a brief historical sketch of technology at the university over the past five to six years. Identify the technology investments and advancements, including what is currently used in the classrooms and throughout the campus.

Lessons Learned. Technology has successes (such as practicality and productivity) as well as failures (such as cost overruns). This section briefly describes what the institution has learned—both the good and the bad—from its use of technology.

National Trends/External Picture. This section identifies what is happening across the country. For example: What new software has been introduced recently? What are other universities using? How do other institutions deal with technology challenges, costs, and funding? What is coming down the road? Such external information helps paint a complete picture of the issue by placing it in context.

Strategic Themes. What critical issues must stakeholders understand (such as business continuity, identity management, and cost of software)? Assume that the reader does not know much about technology and needs to be educated.

Options. Given the rapid pace of change associated with technology, what alternative scenarios should the institution consider? What decisions will need to be made in the future? In this section, also address the "choice points" for the university and the plusses and minuses of various options.

Projected Costs. Estimate the cost of maintaining and improving the technology infrastructure: How much consulting support is anticipated? Who maintains and enhances the system? Are more people needed? How much will hardware and software cost?

Short- and Long-Term Plans. Outline what needs to be done in the next year, which significant changes can be anticipated, and what investments will need to be made over the next several years.

ADVICE FOR CONCEPT PAPER CHAIRS

Concept papers usually take about a month to produce. To get people moving as quickly as possible, convene a face-to-face meeting of your group within one week of the Sensemaking Meeting. The agenda should include clarifying roles, agreeing on expectations, and establishing time frames.

Also provide your team's members with a copy of the Talent Bank created during the two-day CSP training session (see Chapter 3). They can tap some of these people as they complete their assignments.

The sooner the team begins to draft the concept paper, the better. Then you'll have more time to refine ideas, add new information, and make the changes necessary to produce a quality product. For everyone's peace of mind, avoid scrambling at the last minute to put something together right before the deadline. Typically, it will take several meetings or phone conferences for each team's members to get organized, share their initial thinking about the paper, and create a quality product.

NOTES TO PTF CO-CHAIRS

As the writing of the concept papers gets underway, frequently contact the chair of each paper for a progress report. You should have the final say, in consultation with each writing team, on the final version of each concept paper.

Additional suggestions include:

- Ask the chairs of the writing team who they plan to solicit for help, to ensure they aren't overwhelming a select few with requests for assistance. You might even need to negotiate with the chairs to spread assignments equitably among people in the Talent Bank.
- Post all concept papers on the internal planning Web site so PTF members can review the drafts and provide feedback and suggestions. Such transparency builds a sense of ownership for the concept papers and greatly improves the quality of the final products.
- If possible, convene a PTF meeting—preferably a working lunch or dinner—to review all of the concept papers before the vision conference takes place (see Chapter 6). Bring the different concept papers into one holistic discussion and solicit PTF members' general reactions to the papers and the implications of what they have learned. (Invite the president, too.) During this meeting of two hours or so, also review the logistics of the upcoming Vision Conference.

Planning Assumptions

Another outcome of the Sensemaking Meeting is for the PTF members to generally agree on the assumptions that undergird the institution's planning efforts. Planning assumptions help create a shared understanding about how the PTF members and others see the world now and when they look to the future.

A sub-group of the PTF, along with one of the co-chairs, should be charged with creating a short internal document (two to four pages in length) that describes the world in which the institution operates and the one it might inhabit in the future. More specifically, planning assumptions

- Are temporary estimates of your environment over which you have no control
- Are *not* facts
- Identify the elements and forces that *could* impact the organization
- Identify powerful trends that you should pay attention to
- Are general (not detailed) pictures of the current and possible future world
- Help avoid "blue sky" or wishful thinking (such as high student enrollment when the number of high school students is dramatically declining)

This document is best created after the Sensemaking Meeting because the PTF members will have agreed on the main strategic themes and started writing concept papers for the vision conference (see Chapter 6). However, don't use the planning assumptions at the Vision Conference because they offer too much information for participants to absorb at that time. Use them instead at the Goals Conference (see Chapter 7), when the PTF and other relevant insiders create strategic goals and action plans to implement the vision. If you are pressed for time, you can even create the planning assumptions after the Vision Conference.

SOURCES OF INFORMATION

To make good decisions about an issue, people need to understand what is going on locally, regionally, nationally, and internationally concerning the issue. That's why each concept paper should contain the external picture for each issue or strategic theme it covers.

PTF members may find the following resources helping when writing their concept papers.

- The National Association of College and University Business Officers (NACUBO) provides information about the business side of higher education, including results of periodic surveys (on endowments, for example) and reports on the annual Forum for the Future of Higher Education, which addresses high-level trends; www.nacubo.org.
- The College and University Professional Association for Human Resources (CUPA-HR) periodically produces a report on trends influencing higher education, such as its *Think Tank Report on the Future of Higher Education*; www.cupahr.org.
- Each year, the National Center for Education Statistics produces a report detailing enrollment projections for elementary, secondary, and degree-granting institutions; http://nces.ed.gov.
- EDUCAUSE offers information not only on technology issues in higher education but also on a host of other strategic issues; www.educause.edu.

Before participants decide on the set of strategic goals, they need to understand the assumptions on which the planning is based. That way, the goals are created by informed stakeholders' understanding of the world and are connected to reality.

The concept papers will inform the planning assumptions, but they will not be enough. Some limited research will need to take place to craft the right assumptions for your institution. The following text provides a sense of what the planning assumptions document might look like; it is not intended as a comprehensive example.

Economic

- Inflation will remain under 4 percent.
- Health costs will continue to significantly outpace inflation.
- Funding decisions about higher education will be influenced by the tension among access, affordability, and assessment outcomes.
- Unemployment in this region will be 2+ percent higher than most of the rest of the country.
- State budgets will continue to give less to universities like ours.

Social

- The increase in diversity will continue to be a major fact of life for the country and higher education institutions.
- Women's attendance at colleges and universities will continue to increase dramatically.

- The aging of the American population will have a significant impact on society and higher education.
- Increasing social/health/personal problems will continue, and higher education will be expected (sometimes by law) to assume responsibility in dealing with these issues.

Technology

- Career paths in most organizations will demand technological competence from employees.
- Distance learning activities, including hybrid and blended course offerings, will multiply.
- Emerging technology will bring significant challenges to traditional faculty roles in the teaching-learning paradigm.
- The speed of change in technology will increase student expectations, raise costs, and accelerate obsolescence.

Demographics

- The number of high school students in our region will decline by 15 percent over the next five years.
- The adult population will continue to constitute more than 50 percent of college enrollments nationally.
- The fastest growing segment of the population seeking education will be adults searching for retraining or second careers.
- The college-going population will bring increasing challenges to provide access to students with disabilities and those economically disadvantaged.
- Many of the returning vets from the Iraq war will be going to college.

Competition

- The changing image of our city will provide a more marketable location.
- Regional graduate school enrollment is expected to increase by 20 percent over the next several years as employers expect a more skilled workforce.
- Several of our local competitors (e.g., Incredible University, Byrne College) are improving their overall academic reputation dramatically.
- Student indebtedness will be a deciding factor on admission decisions.

Political/Legal

- The national political environment will depict higher education as a national resource to be regulated.
- State and federal support for higher education will be contingent on account-ability.
- Financial aid regulations will continue to become more complex and contain biases against non-traditional students.

chapter 6

PHASE IV— VISION CONFERENCE

The Vision Conference brings together internal and external stakeholders to create a shared picture of the future. This highly interactive, one-day meeting involves 50 to 75 stakeholders. Most of them (60 percent to 70 percent) are internal stakeholders, including all of the Planning Task Force (PTF) members; the others (30 percent to 40 percent) are external stakeholders, such as community leaders, businesspeople, and alumni. Inviting external stakeholders ensures that you have a broader perspective in the room as the institution envisions its future.

The Vision Conference is a powerful community event often remembered by participants for a long time. When you bring together a diverse group of stakeholders who care about the institution and craft a compelling vision of its future, you have a historic moment. (With a large, complex institution, you should convene several one-day Vision Conferences rather than holding a large one with more than 100 participants.)

A Vision Conference has three distinct portions: The Collaborative Teaching Design, Stakeholder Review, and Creating a Preferred Future. It begins with a personal welcome from the president, followed by self-introductions (names and roles) so all participants can get a sense of who else is in the room.

Next, the conference facilitator shares the conference's purposes and reviews the ground rules for the day. These may include:

- One person talks at a time when participants are working in small groups
- Active listening is helpful
- Raise your hand to be acknowledged in the large group discussions

Collaborative Teaching Design
Level of Difficulty: Challenging
Estimated Time: 2½ hours

This design is also called the Jigsaw because it puts together different elements (information) like pieces of a puzzle. For the Vision Conference, you'll use the Collaborative Teaching Design to review the concept papers, educate participants about the key issues, and engage people's thinking. In the end, all the strategic information comes together to provide participants with a coherent and strategic view of the institution.

This design carefully manages information overload, leverages participants' time, and gets everyone on the same page in an efficient manner. It has three distinct parts:

- Participants read an assigned concept paper and distill meaning from it
- Participants are placed in groups where all concept papers are represented to discuss the contents and implications for the institution
- Participants communicate the essential information to the large group for discussion

Logistics

Materials needed: Concept papers for everyone, flipcharts, easels, markers

Space needs: Large, comfortable room with moveable chairs

Facilitator's Directions

Using 50 participants and five concept papers as an example, create five groups of 10 participants.

— Have participants divide into groups by counting off from one to five. People should not sit wherever they wish; they will tend to sit with friends and colleagues, which can hinder cross-boundary discussion. Authors of concept papers may serve as experts in their groups.

The room would look like this:

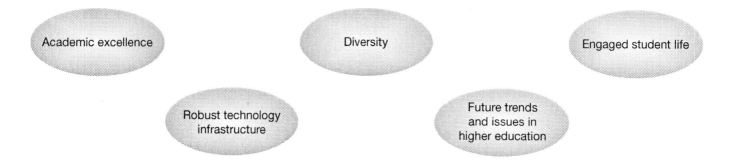

— Once people are assigned to their appropriate table, make sure they identify self-managed roles (see Appendix A) to help organize their efforts. For this part of the design, each group will need a facilitator and a timekeeper.

— Instruct each group to read its assigned concept paper and generally agree on the top four to six key themes—the ideas that are essential to understand as they think about the future of the institution. Although participants can use a flipchart to capture their ideas on paper, also tell them to take notes about the agreed-upon key themes; in the next part of the design, they will share these notes with other attendees.

— Give the groups 30 minutes to read the concept paper and produce a shared list of the key ideas it contains.

— Ask participants to again count off from one to five (because you have five concept papers) and move to the table that corresponds to their new group. This redistributes all the concept paper groups to the newly constituted groups, which now have two representatives from each concept paper. A reconstituted group should look like this:

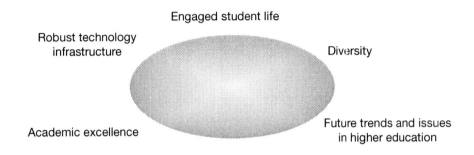

Engaged student life

Robust technology infrastructure

Diversity

Academic excellence

Future trends and issues in higher education

— The next round brings all the information together into a coherent whole. Once again, ask the groups to identify their self-managed roles before beginning their discussion. For this part of the design, each group will need a facilitator, timekeeper, presenter, and recorder.

—Let the two people from each concept paper who have carried over from the first round share their most important ideas from their earlier discussion (which is why they'll need to take notes). Give each pair between five and eight minutes to present their ideas. You can leave several minutes for questions and answers, but everyone should finish sharing ideas about all five concept papers in about 45 minutes.

— Next, give each group 10 minutes to generate a list of the most critical information from all five content areas. Suggest that they limit this list to four, five, or six key ideas, which should be recorded on a flipchart.

— Take a 15-minute break at this point because participants have been sitting and thinking for an hour and a half. During the break, organize the flipcharts in the front of the room so that presentations can take place immediately after everyone returns.

— Conclude the Collaborative Teaching Design by asking each group to give a brief presentation on the most important ideas identified. Because there will be a fair amount of common ground, have each presenter share two key ideas from their group's presentation. This way, all groups will have something to share and feel as if their work contributed to the conference. Make as many rounds as necessary to gather all the ideas in the room.

FACILITATOR'S TIP

When you ask people to agree on the top key ideas from all the information, suggest that they consider the ideas "that are essential for us to remember as we think about the future. By essential, we mean that if we don't include these ideas in our thinking, we will not be able to create a meaningful picture of the future."

— After each group has presented, conduct an open discussion with the entire group to bring closure to the design. Limit this discussion to 10 minutes so people do not go off on conversational tangents. To stimulate the group discussion, ask a provocative question or two. For example:

- As you listened to the key ideas, what resonated most with you?
- Were there any surprises or discoveries?
- What had most meaning for you personally?
- What is essential to remember?

— Take a short stretch break (five minutes), then move right into the next part of the Vision Conference.

The Stakeholder Review
Level of Difficulty: Easy
Estimated Time: 45 minutes

The more conference participants understand how different people see their institution, the smarter they become about the complexity of their college or university. To create a well-informed picture of the future, everyone at the conference needs to understand a wide range of data and perspectives.

With the Stakeholder Review, participants organize themselves into their specific stakeholder group (faculty, students, administration, and so forth) and share their unique perspectives to stimulate thinking. Stations should be placed throughout the room for different stakeholder groups. The room should look like this:

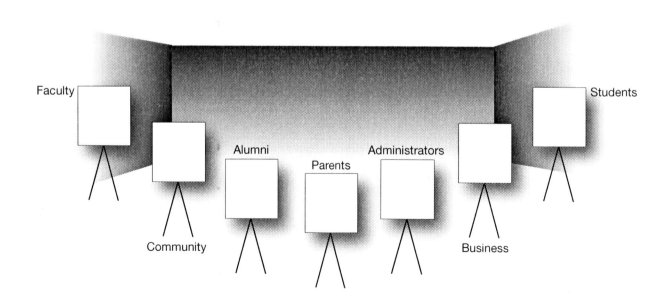

Facilitator's Directions

— Explain the task as follows: "In the next 15 to 20 minutes, talk with one another and discuss these questions:

- From your unique perspective, what is important for us to know about how you see the future of the institution?
- What do you want us to remember as we plan for the future of this place?"

— Give each stakeholder group 20 minutes to discuss and agree on the five most important themes or ideas they want to share with the others in the room. They should put these important themes on a flip chart so everyone can see them. Instruct the groups to use self-managed roles for this activity: Each group will need a facilitator, presenter, recorder, and timekeeper.

— Each stakeholder group should share its five top themes with the whole group. After each brief presentation, ask if anyone has questions *for clarification only*. (This is not a time for debate or contrary opinions.) If a stakeholder group shares information that someone doesn't understand, then clarification is needed, but no one should judge the quality of the ideas or a group's perspective.

Here are some examples of different stakeholder perspectives:

Faculty

- We must make sure that the core curriculum is of the highest quality and at the center of a student's educational experience.
- If we are going to truly embrace diversity, we need to infuse it throughout the curriculum.

Students

- We want more faculty contact; the advising system needs to be improved.
- Campus life on the weekends needs to be much more interesting.
- We want to do directed community service, where we see the impact of our contributions.

Community

- We need you to continue to be a good neighbor and allow community members to attend campus events.
- Many of our local students need mentoring and tutoring; please help us with this.

Business

- We need graduates who can relate well to people and work on teams.
- We need help with research on marketing, technology, and the environment.

FACILITATOR'S TIP

If you have a large number (15 to 20) in a particular stakeholder group, split them into two groups so the Stakeholder Review assignment is more manageable and can be completed in the time allotted. Even if you have a small group (2 to 4 people) of particular stakeholders, make sure they have a discussion and present their information to the whole group. It is not the number of participants that counts, it is their perspectives.

— After all the stakeholder groups have presented, conduct an open group discussion about the important themes that emerged. Keep this discussion to 10 or 15 minutes, and then seek closure on this part of the conference.

Creating a Preferred Future
Level of Difficulty: Moderately challenging
Estimated Time: 1 hour

During the Vision Conference, participants spend a great deal of time understanding the issues facing the institution, listening to one another's unique perspectives, and having cross-boundary conversations. The stage is set for crafting a vision for the future. The Vision Conference culminates with a design that creates a shared picture of the future, five years from now. (The notion of creating a Preferred Future comes from Ron Lippitt and Ed Lindeman, who were seminal thinkers in the organizational development arena during the 1960s.)

Facilitator's Directions

— Provide the following instructions to participants: "Imagine that we are all back in this same room *five years from now*. We are here to celebrate all the successes of our university. We have met many challenges, worked very hard, and accomplished great things. We are in a better place in many ways. People are excited to be on campus, take pride in the institution, and are fully committed to our values and vision. Please answer the focus questions *as if they have already occurred*. Remember: You are looking back five years from now and describing what things look like."

FINDING YOUR FOCUS

Before the vision conference begins, the Planning Task Force needs to agree on a set of focus questions to guide the part related to creating a preferred future. Most of these questions are derived from the concept paper themes because they help organize the essential issues for the entire planning process. And, to a great extent, the concept papers cover the broad strategic areas about which you want to create shared pictures.

Aim for about six focus questions; if you have more than six, participants will experience information overload. Here are several examples of focus questions:

- How is diversity truly lived throughout the institution?
- Please describe the vibrancy of student life. What do you actually see on campus?
- What are students saying or doing?
- What does campus communication look like? What mechanisms, vehicles, or protocols have been put in place to ensure effective, cross-boundary communication?
- What is the role of technology within the institution? How does it serve the teaching and research mission of our university?
- What one institutional accomplishment do you feel especially proud about?
- Is there something we have to change to help us accomplish our goals?
- How do outsiders view us? Our competitors? Students? Community?

— Give participants 15 minutes to think by themselves and answer the focus questions. This way, when they go into their assigned group, they are prepared for the discussion rather than just brainstorming ideas.

— Create 10 diverse groups of five participants each by counting off from one to 10. Ensure that each group has an equal set of participants. Your typical group might look like this:

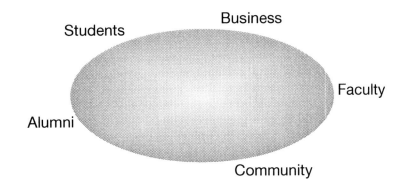

— Instruct the groups to use self-managed roles for this activity. Each group will need a facilitator, presenter, recorder, and timekeeper.

— Have each person in a group share his or her individual picture of the future, based on the focus questions. After each person has spoken, the group needs to create a shared picture of the future based on either common ground or gentle agreement.

Common ground refers to those ideas and themes that members of the group have in common. Typically, there will be many of these because the participants have created a shared database with the concept paper distillation and the sharing of the stakeholder perspectives.

Gentle agreement occurs when an individual in a group offers an idea not common with others but nonetheless interesting and attractive to everyone else in the group. Even though the other group members didn't come up with the idea themselves, they see the sense of it, find it compelling, and believe it adds value. With gentle agreement, however, everyone in the group must generally agree that the idea is worthy of their commitment and would truly help the institution move positively forward. If one or two people disagree with the unique or different idea, it does not go into the shared picture for the group.

— Give each group 60 minutes to share their individual pictures and create a group picture. During that time, quietly check in with each group to see how things are going. Intervene if appropriate—for example, if the group gets stuck on a question or one member starts to dominate the discussion.

FACILITATOR'S TIP

Pay attention to when each group starts to use the flipcharts to create its Preferred Future. Some groups will start writing on the flipchart almost immediately. Others will remain engrossed in discussion. Remind participants at the half-time mark (30 minutes) to begin using the flipcharts. If necessary, issue another reminder at the 45-minute mark. You want to avoid the situation in which most of the groups have finished their shared pictures but one or two are just starting right before the allotted time is up. The slowpokes can slow down the entire process.

— Have participants take a 10-minute stretch break. At this point, you'll have 10 group pictures—too many for participants to comprehend. It is essential that these get condensed to five pictures because 10 are just too much to comprehend and there will be too much redundancy in the presentations. The groups that would go last are penalized because participants simply won't be very interested in their presentations.

— To condense the 10 pictures to five, ask each group to pair up with another group and present their shared pictures to one another. This should take about 10 minutes total (five minutes per group):

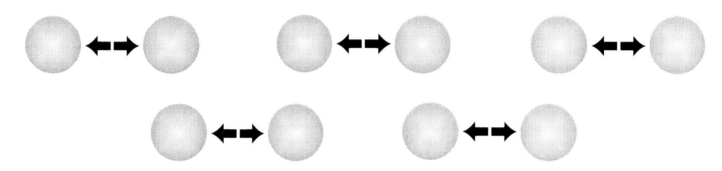

— Now, give the larger groups (10 participants each) about 30 minutes to incorporate the ideas of their previous smaller groups into a shared picture that represents their best thinking. Again, the groups should use the ideas of common ground and gentle agreement. Remind them that if one group offers a gentle agreement idea and the other group disagrees with it, that idea doesn't go into the shared picture.

— Ask each larger group to present its shared picture to the entire group. Allocate five minutes per group.

— After all the presentations have concluded, have a brief closing discussion about people's reactions and responses to the shared pictures. (Typically, they will make positive comments.)

— Have the president or appropriate leader (such as the board chair) thank everyone for participating. The closing remarks should include a reminder that copies of the shared pictures will be available online in about a week (or sent directly to participants, if they prefer).

Drafting a Vision Statement

Following the Vision Conference, members of the Planning Task Force need to take responsibility for integrating all of the shared pictures into a draft of a vision statement. A process will need to be established so the task force can share the draft with conference participants—and other campus stakeholders—and solicit their reactions and feedback.

NOTES TO PTF CO-CHAIRS

It's not unusual for task force members to experience a psychological letdown after the intensity and success of the Vision Conference. But the last phase of the planning process—the Goals Conference—still remains to be conducted.

Pay special attention to this transition time from vision to goals by scheduling face-to-face interaction with PTF members. For instance, hold a celebratory lunch or breakfast meeting to keep PTF members engaged and to share the logistics of the upcoming Goals Conference.

Beyond sharing the draft vision statement on the campus Web site, the task force should hold a series of interactive meetings throughout the campus to obtain feedback and build ownership among various groups. Some institutions, for example, film a presentation of the draft vision statements from the Vision Conference presentations to share with alumni, community members, parents, students, and stakeholders who didn't attend the vision conference. Although you'll need to provide some context before others view the video, the vision statement presentations will still communicate passion and aspiration.

This process of gathering feedback on the vision should take somewhere between two and four weeks. If it takes longer, you run the risk of losing people's interest and losing momentum in the planning process. During this process, the Value Statement should also be shared and feedback encouraged. When stakeholders see both the Vision and Values statement, they experience a coherent and aligned picture of the future. This tends to be a powerful and evocative experience.

The following examples of vision statements come from two very different institutions. They'll give you an idea of what a vision statement might look like.

Incredible University Vision Statement (5-Year Picture)

Incredible University is an emerging, premier institution in the region. We are known for our academic excellence, innovation, scholarship, and caring community. We live our institutional values and guiding principles every day in service to our mission, our students, and the communities we serve.

Our students are engaged and engaging. They are recognized for their leadership skills, ethical behavior, rigorous thinking, and the contributions they make to society. They are proud to be at Incredible University, and we are proud of them.

We are financially sound and greatly improving. We allocate our resources wisely. We have developed the capacity to make difficult decisions and tough choices. Our campus is a beautiful and welcoming place.

We have developed several well-known, flagship programs and are committed to excellence in everything we do. Our faculty is excellent. Teaching in the classroom is first rate, and our leadership is visionary and compassionate. We have a deep sense of who we are and where we are going.

University of the West Indies (UWI) Vision Statement

In 2012, the University of the West Indies is recognized as a world-class research and teaching institution. The UWI degree is the standard of excellence in undergraduate education in the region.

Our graduates are work-ready and distinguished by being exceptionally well-grounded in their disciplines, articulate, possessed of superior problem-solving and critical-thinking skills, and the ability to work effectively in teams. They are socially conscious, civic minded, and committed to ethical behavior.

We are responsive to national needs yet retain a strong regional character. Mechanisms are in place to facilitate continuous dialogue with national stakeholders. We have proactively addressed the needs of the UWI-12 and other underserved stakeholders. We are *the* source for research, expertise, and solutions in dealing with the complex issues and challenges facing the region.

Our financial health is stable and sustainable because of diverse funding sources and strong support from our contributing countries. We have dramatically improved our administrative systems and processes. They are user-friendly, integrated, efficient, and effective.

Major changes have been made in our curriculum and the way we teach. Technology infuses our learning environment and expands the range of quality academic programs we offer. Our students move seamlessly through the entire university to achieve their educational goals.

Our institutional culture is defined by courageous and effective leadership, a results orientation, rigorous accountability, and a deep sense of humanity. We value our people and reward excellence. We are an innovative and modern university deeply rooted in the traditions of the Caribbean, committed to creating the best possible future for all our stakeholders.

chapter 7

PHASE V—
GOALS CONFERENCE

The Goals Conference provides the first opportunity for the Planning Task Force (PTF), the president, and other relevant insiders to decide what actions need to be taken to start implementing the plan.

As they think about the broad goals for each strategic theme, they'll draw on the concept papers, which all participants should have read when they participated in the Vision Conference (or in preparation for the Goals Conference). They'll also refer to the planning assumptions generated after the Sensemaking Meeting (see Chapter 5). These assumptions will give everyone at the Goals Conference a shared picture of the current and anticipated world the institution inhabits. They will ground participants in the realities of the day and encourage the creation of powerful goals for the future.

Participants should include all task force members, plus other key people whose buy-in is critical to the success of the plan's implementation—such as the human resources director, director of physical plant, development officers, student life directors, and so forth. The president's entire senior team or cabinet must attend because their participation and real involvement are crucial at this stage of the process.

Although 20 or 30 new faces may be present at the Goals Conference, everyone in the room should have been a part of the planning process from the beginning. This is why data gathering and engagement (Phase II) are so important: Stakeholders already feel well-informed and prepared because their opinions have been solicited and listened to, and effective and transparent communication has occurred throughout the CSP. The Vision Conference has created an informed and shared picture of the institution's future.

In short, the stage has been set for everyone attending the Goals Conference to fully participate in crafting the beginning of an implementation plan. Note the word *beginning*. The main purpose of the Goals Conference is to create a broad, not detailed, implementation plan. Ideally, conference participants will achieve general agreement on four or five goals related to each of the strategic themes that were agreed to during the Sensemaking Meeting and developed at the Vision Conference.

SUGGESTED SCHEDULE FOR GOALS CONFERENCE

Welcome by president and co-chairs	10 minutes
Consultant/facilitator shares goals and purposes for the day	10 minutes
Brief review of the planning assumptions	10–15 minutes
Attendees self-select a strategic theme to work on, using self-managed groups, and craft beginning goals for each theme	30 minutes
Take an official break	10 minutes
Each self-selected group presents its suggested goals, and the large group prioritizes them	60 minutes
Take an official break	15 minutes
Self-selected groups create detailed action plans for their two top-priority goals	60 minutes
Lunch break	60–75 minutes
Each self-selected group presents its two prioritized action plans with constructive feedback provided	60–75 minutes
Take an official break	15 minutes
Each strategic theme group incorporates feedback and creates refined action plans	45 minutes
Each strategic theme group makes brief presentations to the larger group	60 minutes
President and co-chairs communicate about next steps and share expectations and assignments	30 minutes
Closing comments by president and co-chairs	10 minutes
TOTAL:	8 ½ hours

Goals Conference
Level of Difficulty: Moderate
Estimated Time: 8½ Hours

The full-day Goals Conference begins with the president and PTF co-chairs welcoming participants, thanking them for their participation, and emphasizing how important their work will be to the entire collaborative strategic process. For new attendees, a brief description of the process to date would be helpful.

Facilitator's Directions

— Review how the day will unfold so everyone understands the journey they will be taking.

— Review the planning assumptions document, explaining how it was created and who the co-authors were. This is *not* a time for debate about the planning assumptions, which the PTF has already approved.

— Ask participants to self-select one of the strategic themes (such as student life, academic excellence, or diversity) they would like to work on. Emphasize that participants will be discussing and generally agreeing on a set of proposed goals for their strategic theme area.

— Once participants have formed groups around strategic themes, ask them to use self-managed roles to help support their discussion (see Appendix A). Give them 30 minutes to generally agree on four or five goals for their strategic area. Remind everyone to refer to the concept papers, the vision statement, and the planning assumptions as they create their goals.

— Ask each group to report its initial thinking about a set of goals for that particular strategic theme. Each presentation should take no more than five minutes, followed by a two-minute period for questions of clarification.

Here's an example of goals related to a strategic theme:

Engaged Student Life
- Create a Freshman Experience program to help entering freshmen transition to the campus and keep them
- Create community service opportunities as part of the graduation requirements
- Have a visiting speakers program that attracts national-level speakers to the campus
- Refurbish the Student Center and make it wireless
- Reinvest in the Student Scholars program and improve its quality and attractiveness to students
- Create a Division III football program

— After each group has made its presentation, have participants use the Las Vegas Voting design (See Appendix A) to prioritize the goals for each strategic theme. (Do not wait until all the presentations are over to do this; people will find the task too overwhelming and you'll lose momentum.) After each presentation, give participants one dot to place on the goal they believe will help move that strategic theme forward.

— After all the presentations and voting have taken place, take a 15- or 20-minute break. At this point, participants will be using their time and talent where they want to, you'll have some thoughtful goals suggested by interested and informed participants, and you'll have prioritized the beginning goals with full participation of all attendees in a transparent manner.

— After the break, ask participants to return to their strategic theme area and work on the top two goals. Remind them to use self-managed roles. For each goal, they should craft a beginning action plan that follows this format:

- Goal statement
- Three important steps toward implementing the goal
- Resources needed (people, money, technology, office space, and so forth)
- Time frame for implementing each step
- Suggested champion or owner—the person who will be ultimately responsible for the successful completion of the goal
- Who needs to be involved in the successful implementation of the three important steps
- A description of what success would look like
- Potential hurdles or challenges that would prevent implementation

Make sure the groups stay on task and don't delve into too much detail. Schedule a 60- or 70-minute block of time for creating action plans for both goals; if you provide more time, the day will drag on and the entire group will lose momentum. You might give attendees a 30-minute warning with chimes or a bell so they can pace themselves accordingly.

— After the groups have created their two action plans, have them take a 15-minute break.

— When they return from the break, the groups should take turns presenting their two action plans. Leave a minute or so after each plan has been presented to answer questions *for clarification only*, not for debate or discussion. About halfway through the action plan presentations, take a 10-minute break to sustain energy.

— After each group has presented its action plans, provide everyone with a stack of Post-it notes and have them use the Constructive Feedback design (see Appendix A). Their feedback should respond to these questions:

- What do you like about the suggested action plan steps?
- What advice do you have to improve the action plan?
- What resources can you share that would help with the action plan implementation (such as research, available grant money, your own expertise in an area, the expertise of someone you know, or other institutions that have accomplished something similar)?

— Give participants a 15-minute break to reenergize after all the presentations have concluded.

— Next, each strategic theme group should incorporate the constructive feedback received from the other participants into refined action plans. Allocate about 45 minutes for this task. Their goal is not to completely rewrite their action plans but to review the feedback and meaningfully incorporate the ideas into a final version. Most groups will have plenty of feedback, but they should guard against getting bogged down in details or feeling as if they have to incorporate every idea.

— Give each strategic theme group a second opportunity to share its action plans with all attendees. Keep these presentations to five minutes each. The goal is to share how the feedback influenced and helped refine the draft action plans. No discussion period is necessary after these action plan presentations. To keep things moving, monitor time carefully and make sure one group or presenter doesn't give a long-winded presentation.

— Halfway through the final action plan presentations, take a 10-minute break.

— Following all of the presentations, the president or PTF co-chairs need to emphasize that each strategic theme group should organize its action plans and put them in electronic format *within one week*. The completed action plans, which will form the foundation for the implementation plan, should be sent to the PTF co-chairs for review. The president also needs to outline the process the cabinet will follow for reviewing the other suggested goals that were not developed during the conference; attendees work only on the top two priority goals. Whatever the process proposed by the president, it should not come as a surprise to the PTF members that the cabinet's ownership of the implementation plan is critical to its success.

— Have the president and PTF co-chairs thank all the attendees for their hard work and answer any questions about the next steps.

> **FACILITATOR'S TIP**
>
> During the goals conference, schedule breaks as appropriate to the group's pace, complexity, and peculiarity—not necessarily according to the suggested agenda. The goals conference is an intense day featuring a lot of thinking and discussion. Do whatever it takes to keep things moving, whether that's numerous mini-breaks, healthy food, or even entertainment at lunch time.

Drafting the Implementation Plan

The PTF is responsible for creating a collaborative planning process for the institution. For the most part, its job is complete when the Goals Conference concludes. The cabinet needs to own the next steps in the process because that body is responsible for implementing the strategic plan as well as running the university. Only the cabinet fully understands the complexity of all the operations, initiatives, and projects currently in place and knows the most appropriate and effective ways to integrate the goals into everything already occurring on campus.

Many cabinet members undoubtedly serve on the PTF, in part to ensure buy-in to the planning outcomes. They have been present from the beginning, both informing and being informed by the process, and building trust among other PTF members. The cabinet is poised to own the process going forward because these people understand how the vision, goals, and action plans have been created and have been able to influence the outcomes of the plan.

After the conference, the cabinet—in consultation with the president—reviews the remaining goals and decides how to integrate them into the plan *over time*. There is no way all the suggested goals will be implemented; this fact needs to be made clear to all participants in the Goals Conference. First, the institution must put its efforts toward accomplishing the prioritized goals as quickly and reasonably as possible.

Here are several suggestions for this stage:

- Throughout the process of creating the implementation plan, the cabinet should remain committed to the guiding principles of inclusivity, transparency, and honesty.

- The president should allocate between 30 and 45 days to working with the cabinet to review the goals and action plans and to present a proposed implementation plan to the entire PTF.
- After creating the implementation plan, the president and cabinet should reconvene the PTF for a lunch or dinner meeting to explain the rationale for the plan and invite feedback. After this open and interactive meeting, which usually features a lot of discussion and debate, implementation of the planning process begins.
- The PTF should reconvene periodically for updates on progress and the challenges regarding the plan. At a minimum, the task force should meet with the cabinet once a year for collegial discussion and dialogue.

Once finalized, the implementation plan should appear on the campus intranet so all stakeholders can view it and provide feedback. The implementation plan should not be mysterious in any way. Stakeholders should know not only the priority goals but also the action plans that support them.

IMPLEMENTATION

Collaborative Strategic Planning (CSP) focuses primarily on the process behind the strategic plan because that's typically where strategic planning breaks down. The five-phase model helps create a shared picture of the future that stakeholders are committed to achieving.

While commitment is essential, it is not enough. The reason to craft a collaborative planning process is to implement the plan. Doing so enables the institution to achieve its hopes and aspirations. Without implementation, all the engagement, interest, ideas, and goodwill will come to nothing.

Increasing the Likelihood of Success

There is no silver bullet or recommended model to solve the implementation challenge. Each institution is different, its culture unique, its leadership capacity varied, its history complex, and its execution mentality either strong or weak (or somewhere in between).

Some well-known methods are based on linear thinking and project management models but do not account for systemic change. Gantt charts, critical path methods, financial modeling, and a host of other tools can certainly be helpful, but none can drive the implementation process. Only people—with all of their quirks, interests, passions, energy, and hopes—can implement strategic plans.

With that thought in mind, here is some advice that has grown out of the experience of numerous educational institutions. These suggestions do not appear in priority order—that would be linear thinking—but they provide an information base for leaders interested in collaborative planning and implementation.

Appoint many cabinet members to serve on the Planning Task Force (PTF). This ensures their deep understanding of, and connection to, the planning process. Avoid a situation in which the president's cabinet inherits a strategic plan with which they have no connection.

Gone are the days when a group creates a strategic plan without meaningfully involving and engaging the people who will actually put that plan into action. One essential element of CSP is the direct involvement of many institutional leaders in crafting the plan, engaging stakeholders, making sense of the data collected, and envisioning the institution's future.

Conduct a planning audit. Before embarking on CSP, the cabinet and all PTF members should complete the audit, which assesses an institution's capacity to do strategic planning (see Appendix E). The results of this informal, anonymous survey will give leaders deep insight into planning strengths and weaknesses.

The audit asks about campus communication and collaboration but, more important, it asks about the institution's internal ability to plan, its ability to get things done, and its ability to measure performance toward stated goals. These are all implementation questions. Armed with the results, leadership can begin to put in place the protocols and mechanisms that will ensure the results of the CSP are implemented.

Strike a balance between attempting too much and too little. At the end of the CSP, you have a five-year, shared picture of the institution's future, plus specific goals and action plans to implement. Initially, people will show great enthusiasm for getting things done. This sense of urgency creates momentum and high expectations, leading stakeholders to take on far too much during the first year. Consequently, they become overwhelmed and frustrated, and implementation stalls.

The cabinet and PTF should discuss this potential pitfall openly to avoid trying to cram 85 percent of the plan's implementation into the first year. Remember, it is a five-year plan. Focus on a few important items, not everything, and move forward on those.

Instead of tackling too much at the start, some institutions take the opposite approach and don't implement any part of the plan after CSP concludes. This "planning to plan" mentality plagues many educational institutions, such as the one that engaged in strategic planning for 14 years without moving to the implementation phase. The school was, as one faculty member stated, "a large battleship, in a lagoon, in a fog."

Typically, this phenomenon emerges in the writing of the plan. In the plan's first year you will see language such as "do extensive and comprehensive research about the competition/student demographics/best practices/curriculum renewal," followed in the second year by phrases such as "analyze the data and draft actions for review." If you wait until the third year of plan to implement anything, you will lose momentum. Plus, the world will have changed dramatically in the intervening years.

Collaborative strategic planning creates commitment and generates a lot of information and ideas. After the Goals Conference, you already have the beginning of an implementation plan. Obviously, you may need to do further research and analysis—but not about everything. So while research and analysis are underway for some areas, focus on those ideas that can be implemented almost immediately.

Identify an "owner" for each goal area defined through the CSP. Before the CSP begins, the president should communicate to the campus community that a high-level administrator—or, in some cases, a faculty member—will take responsibility for each strategic goal that emerges from the plan. This signals to the campus stakeholders that the president is committed to ensuring implementation of the plan.

Once identified, these "owners" are responsible for the successful implementation of their specific goal. For example, the vice president of student affairs might own a strategic goal related to student life, while the provost might take responsibility for the goal of academic excellence. Obviously, the provost would need the help of the deans and faculty, but the provost alone is responsible and held accountable for the successful implementation of the goal.

This single point of accountability is essential to implementation. Ideally, a chart should identify all of the institution's strategic goals and the owner of each goal. Make this chart public by posting it on the institution's intranet for review by stakeholders. Such clarity and transparency help improve the chances of the plan being implemented.

Each leader responsible for a goal area should provide the president with a summary of his or her current responsibilities and priorities (and the time allocated to each), along with a delegation plan for shifting some responsibilities to others in order to personally focus on implementing the relevant part of the plan. This will show the president that the leader not only thinks strategically but also has developed the capacity for others to take on new responsibilities.

The delegation plan needs to be negotiated with and sanctioned by the president and communicated to cabinet members. The cabinet needs to understand the new roles and responsibilities so they can support the responsible leader's efforts.

Provide the appropriate resources for implementing the action plans. Each leader responsible for a goal area must receive the appropriate resources to implement the action plan related to that area. The leader needs time to think through what needs to be done, garner the appropriate resources, and organize the appropriate people to help with execution.

Although adequate money, people, and technology are all important when implementing a plan's goals, the most valuable resource is time. If busy executives are assigned goal areas to implement on top of all their other responsibilities, the strategic plan will remain on the shelf. Piling more work on a busy leader's time works only in the short run—if at all. These leaders will quickly feel overwhelmed and burdened, which leads to resentfulness and ineffectiveness.

That's why the president must help carve out the time for each leader to participate fully in implementation, possibly by delegating day-to-day business responsibilities to immediate subordinates, reprioritizing the current workload, or reassigning core responsibilities to other competent leaders. Such actions free the senior leaders to apply their talents to moving the plan forward.

Annually update the entire campus on the strategic plan. Updates can take several forms; the most effective is a campus-wide meeting, convened by the president, for reporting progress toward the established strategic goals. The president, cabinet, and PTF co-chairs should invite interested campus stakeholders to a forum that explains the outputs and outcomes of the planning process and asks for feedback and advice.

When progress has been slower than desired—which will definitely happen—the leadership must communicate what they have learned about the problems and how they plan to do a course correction. As long as stakeholders believe that learning is taking place and will inform future actions, they will be somewhat forgiving of the less-than-successful efforts.

Stakeholders appreciate hearing about the problems as well as the successes and being able to engage in constructive, two-way communication. Meeting those needs enhances the

GETTING THE JOB DONE

In *Execution: The Discipline of Getting Things Done*, Larry Bossidy and Ram Charan bring together, respectively, their corporate management experience and scholarship on business leadership to provide advice for any leader who wants results. Although neither author is familiar with the intricacies and complexities of higher education, their book offers observations and ideas that are applicable to any educational institution interested in implementing the strategic goals its stakeholders have so carefully crafted.

As the authors see it, execution remains the largest unaddressed issue in the business world today. Its absence is the single biggest obstacle to success and the reason behind most disappointments that are mistakenly attributed to other causes. They believe that too many leaders place too much emphasis on high-level strategy—on intellectualizing and philosophizing—and not enough on implementation.

In fact, many people regard execution as detail work that's beneath the dignity of a business leader. That's wrong, say Bossidy and Charan. To the contrary, execution is a leader's most important job. They define execution as a discipline and a system, not simply a collection of tactics, built into an organization's strategy, goals, and culture. Most important, the organization's leader must be deeply engaged in this system.

The authors state, "We know of no great leaders, whether in business or politics, military or religion, or any other field, who don't have the personal connections in their organizations." This observation highlights an essential theme in collaborative strategic planning: Relationships, not written documents, are essential to the successful implementation of any plan. People need to feel connected to a greater good, to believe that they can make a difference and advance their institution's future.

PTF's credibility and communicates the values of honesty and transparency. If you have a large campus, hold several of these campus forums, at different times of the day, to ensure widespread participation.

Also make the planning "report card" or "scorecard" available on the campus intranet for interested parties to review.

Periodically reconvene the PTF. The PTF remains a strategic asset for the institution even after a plan is in place. These credible leaders and individuals have helped craft the planning process, deeply understand the institution's strengths and weaknesses, and are committed to successfully implementing the plan.

At least twice a year, the president should reconvene the PTF to discuss how things are going. This enables task force members to help solve problems encountered in a particular goal area, strategically think through the future implications and impacts of an initiative, or provide feedback and advice on proposed actions. PTF members can also participate in annual planning reports made to the community and serve as an internal "accountability group" regarding the plan.

Include the strategic plan on the cabinet's regular agenda. If the president and cabinet don't have a regular (monthly) review of the planning implementation, nothing will happen. Cabinet members should be investing much of their time, thinking, and attention to executing the goals they helped develop.

The strategic plan is not some process running parallel to regular business operations; it must eventually become the institution's regular business. That's why every meeting of the cabinet needs to include both broad and deep discussion about the implementation of strategic goals and actions. Remember: Business as usual simply keeps you in business for the moment. The strategic plan is about thriving *in the future*. Focus your attention on the horizon, and your institution will meet its promise and potential.

In closing, you might find the following design helpful for enhancing the chances of successful implementation.

The Pre-Mortem
Level of Difficulty: Moderate to Challenging
Estimated Time: 2 Hours

A post-mortem is used to reflect on what happened after an event (for example, a death, an organizational failure, or a crisis). In contrast, you use a Pre-Mortem *before* undertaking an action or initiative. First by looking forward, then backward, this design anticipates the potential pitfalls, hurdles, and potholes that may await you so you can strategically deal with the anticipated problems.

After the Goals Conference—or other planning meeting where stakeholders create action plans for implementation—one strategic question must be asked: What could go wrong with this action plan? People tend to avoid this question, especially when they have worked hard to create the action or implementation plan. They want to create momentum by accomplishing something rather than identifying the challenges to success. Anticipating what could go wrong may seem counterintuitive to success, but it helps build strategic thinking and problem-solving skills.

It's best to use this design a few days *after* a group has created an implementation or action plan. That gives the group time to digest their ideas and gain psychological distance from their implementation plans. After a few days, group members can be more objective about their ideas and more open to identifying potential challenges. This design also uses the highly interactive Carousel design to gather and prioritize the best ideas.

Logistics

Materials: Flipcharts, easels, magic markers for everyone, masking tape, timer, chimes, definitions of terms, Carousel Design handout

Space Needs: Large, comfortable room where participants can move around easily, plus a lot of useable wall space

Number of Participants: 10 to 40

The facilitator needs to set up six stations in the room that correspond to the six diagnostic elements. Using 30 participants as the example, create six mixed groups by asking participants to count off from one to six. This produces six groups of five participants each.

The room should look like this:

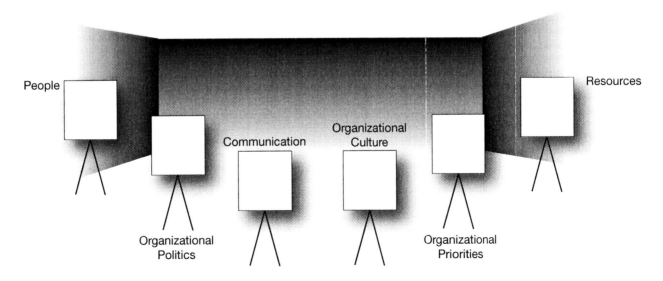

People

Resources

Communication

Organizational
Culture

Organizational
Politics

Organizational
Priorities

Facilitator's Directions

— Welcome participants and explain the purpose of the meeting: "Today we want to anticipate what could go wrong with our action plans *before* we try to implement them."

— Communicate the following: "Imagine we are all back here one year from now. Although we have worked long and hard, we have *failed* to implement our proposed action plans. We are here today to diagnose what went wrong. We are going to look at six specific elements that blocked our successful implementation. They are:

- Organizational politics
- Organizational culture
- Organizational priorities
- Resources (technology, money)
- People
- Communication

BASIC DEFINITIONS

When conducting a Pre-Mortem, it's helpful to offer definitions of the six elements discussed during the design. You may use these definitions or develop your own so participants are clear about the information they need to create.

Organizational politics. This element deals with how decisions are made about what gets done in an organization. This is where *who* wants some things accomplished is more important than *what* needs to be done. It also deals with governance processes and what certain groups (such as faculty senate, trustees, or cabinet) want or don't want.

Organizational culture. This involves the organizational norms and values that influence behavior and decision making. It is "the way things get done around here" yet is rarely explicit. Almost everyone clearly understands what gets rewarded and punished in their organization without openly discussing it.

Organizational priorities. These are the institution's formal and informal goals and objectives. If an action plan is not aligned with where the organization wants to go, it will have many challenges. Problems arise, for example, if the trustees want to accomplish something in contrast to what the faculty or president thinks is possible or relevant. Friction will likely result if the trustees want to have a national presence and the strategic goals are more regionally focused.

Resources. These can be defined as money, technology, leadership attention, time, and physical space—all the elements that are needed to support an action. It is important to think through what needs to be in place to successfully implement a plan.

People. You must have the appropriate number of people necessary to implement an action plan. For example, if you are creating a new academic program, a certain number of faculty are needed to resource it. You also need the right kind of people to implement an action plan. Just having bodies isn't enough—they have to be the right bodies. This element also relates to stakeholders, both internal and external, who can help or hurt the implementation of an action plan.

Communication. Without effective, efficient information sharing, implementation will falter. Communication also has to be transparent and timely. When people don't receive information, they don't feel valued. It's essential to create a variety of communication vehicles (face-to-face, Internet, small and large group meetings, newsletters, and so forth) that help keep people informed.

— Review definitions of the six elements (see sidebar), and communicate the following: "As you work in your groups, please think ahead one year from now and anticipate some of the reasons we were *not* successful. What blocks, challenges, or hurdles can you identify that might have gotten in our way?"

— After ensuring everyone has a marker, instruct the group members to go to the theme corresponding to their number and individually print their answers to the focus question. Participants who agree with someone else's comments should indicate agreement by checking ($\sqrt{}$) the statement. If they don't agree, they make no mark. (This design is about individual data gathering, not group agreement.) This is another version of the Carousel design described earlier in the book.

— After a few minutes, ring the chimes and instruct each group to rotate clockwise to the next station. Participants read the information that has already been written down and individually check off all the ideas with which they agree. They also add their own ideas.

— The rotations continue until each group has provided individual input for all six elements. This will take only 20 to 30 minutes, but will provide the group with a great deal of strategic information. The output might look like this:

ORGANIZATIONAL POLITICS

We never identified the informal leaders who needed to buy into our implementation plan $\sqrt{}\sqrt{}\sqrt{}\sqrt{}$

We never got real buy-in from the faculty union $\sqrt{}\sqrt{}\sqrt{}\sqrt{}$ $\sqrt{}\sqrt{}$

We didn't understand the complexity of the governance process $\sqrt{}\sqrt{}\sqrt{}\sqrt{}$

The trustees weren't educated about the implications of the strategic plan $\sqrt{}\sqrt{}\sqrt{}$

Competing interests on the cabinet stopped any real progress $\sqrt{}\sqrt{}$

— At this stage, you have two options: You can either assign participants to a strategic element or let them self-select an element of personal interest.

— Once the groups have formed, explain the task as follows: "In the next 30 minutes we would like you to come up with some strong recommendations that would effectively deal with the identified challenges for your strategic element. Please use the information we have created to inform your thinking."

— Ring the chime after 30 minutes and ask each group to present its strong recommendations to the larger group for review and feedback. For example, the Organizational Politics presentation might look like this:

We never identified the informal leaders who needed to buy into our implementation plan
- Use the PTF members to identify the list of informal leaders who are essential to helping us succeed with implementing our action plan.
- Invite these informal leaders to a review meeting about our proposed action plan and actively solicit feedback from them. The PTF co-chairs should host and facilitate this meeting.
- Ask these leaders how we can best keep them informed about our progress throughout the implementation process.
- Provide opportunities throughout the implementation process to solicit their ideas and feedback, so this is not a one-shot deal.

We never got real buy-in from the faculty union
- The implementation team for the Academic Excellence action plan needs to sit down with the president of the faculty senate and discuss how they can work together to facilitate the goals.
- Each member of the implementation team needs to get educated about the governance process on this campus.
- We need to schedule updates at the monthly faculty senate about the progress of the action plan.

— After the six presentations have concluded, the group decides who will do what. Having a lot of good ideas isn't enough; people must commit to implementing the ideas. Each diagnostic element needs someone to take ownership of the recommendations and move them forward. This does not mean the "owner" must do everything recommended but should, at the least, identify key people who could help implement the best ideas.

— Reconvene the same group two or three weeks later and report the progress of the recommendations. This communicates that some efforts are already successful, builds a sense of accountability that recommended actions will be paid attention to, and develops the strategic notion that anticipating problems before they occur is a smart move.

Schedule

Facilitator welcomes participants, shares purposes, and reviews definition of terms	10 minutes
Facilitator uses a counting-off method to create six randomly mixed groups	5 minutes
The six groups rotate to all six stations and write down their individual answers for each diagnostic element	25–30 minutes
Groups self-select the diagnostic element they are most interested in and create recommendations	30 minutes
Each group presents their ideas to the large group	20–25 minutes
Open discussion about who will follow through with the recommendations	15–30 minutes
TOTAL:	Approximately 2 hours

chapter 9

10 LESSONS LEARNED

When it comes to implementation, two dangers are inherent in any kind of institution-wide strategic planning process. The first danger: attempting to do far too much during the first year. Remember, you have a five-year plan, and you'll implement the strategies and goals over time. Stuffing too many activities into the beginning of the implementation period simply exhausts people rather than creating energy and momentum.

The second danger comes in the form of the planning-to-plan syndrome that haunts many strategic planning processes, especially within academic institutions. This is manifested in the five-year plan that devotes its first and second years to research, analysis, and thinking about implementation. The result is "analysis paralysis" and a plan that never gets off the ground. Stakeholders throughout the institution have been participating and engaged and will want to accomplish something, so watch the language of the implementation plan. For instance, words such as *implement* and *initiate* should far outnumber words such as *research* and *investigate*.

In addition to remaining aware of—and avoiding—these dangers, you may find comfort, strength, or even inspiration in these 10 lessons learned from other institutions that have fully engaged in collaborative strategic planning.

1. **This is hard work.** Anyone who says otherwise doesn't know what he or she is talking about. To do CSP right, you need committed leadership, dedicated people, a learning attitude, and a lot of human time, attention, and work.

    There are no shortcuts. Once you begin the journey, you are committed for the long haul. You can't stop the process once you have articulated to campus stakeholders what you will be doing. Be conscious of the major commitment your institution will make when it engages in this kind of strategic planning process.

2. **When you do CSP well, you raise the expectations of the internal and external stakeholders.** Once people become meaningfully engaged in a collaborative process, they want to participate in the future thinking about the campus. CSP has lasting effects: Throughout the institution, people will expect greater involvement, shared and transparent information, open communication, participative meetings, collaborative decision making, and a deep sense of institutional community.

3. **CSP is all about relationships, relationships, relationships.** Relationships are the currency of higher education; without constructive and authentic relationships, very little gets done. The relationships developed and nurtured during the collaborative process—especially among the campus leaders and other stakeholders—are the key to the successful implementation of the plan. Once people feel heard and can see both their "fingerprints" and "mindprints" on the plan, they will be committed to implementing it.

4. **Trust is essential to accomplishing anything meaningful.** Leaders throughout the campus need to pay attention to the level of institutional trust and understand how to build and nurture it. The good news is that you can build and sustain trust with a well-defined, inclusive planning process. You build trust by valuing people's ideas, being inclusive in your practices, showing respect for differences, being transparent with decisions, and being deeply honest in your communication.

5. **Planning isn't linear.** It is amazing, if not appalling, that the myth of linear planning exists in most educational institutions. This myth is mostly driven by leaders who have a technical, analytical, and logical mindset. These people believe that 2 + 2 always equals 4, even when little evidence exists. They prefer planning as an information and data-driven process that doesn't take into account people's hopes, aspirations, fears, questions, and doubts.

    This linear approach is an attempt to control the future. Unfortunately, that cannot be done. Responding to and influencing your future, however, is possible when you have high levels of trust, dedicated and committed leaders, good information that people understand, a shared vision for the future, and people willing to work hard.

    Of course, linear thinkers are still needed; they just can't dominate a planning process. You also need visionaries to help craft noble futures, relational people to build a sense of community, and execution-oriented individuals who strive mightily to get things done. In short, different people, different thinking, and different approaches are necessary for a more holistic way of planning together.

6. **It is important to "keep score" throughout the planning and implementation phases.** Routine practices such as "chews and chats" will help update stakeholders about issues throughout the implementation process. Beyond that, every year there should be a series of planning "report outs" where the president and other key leaders communicate progress toward the goals articulated in the plan. This way, campus stakeholders will come to expect regular and honest communication about their efforts toward the institutional goals. Because people like to keep score, they will welcome and find value in a regular scorecard.

    Always communicate shortcomings as well as successes. To stakeholders, bad news is just as important as good news; both build credibility and trust in institutional leadership. As long as the less-than-successful efforts are not blamed on everyone and the leadership conveys what they learned about the lack of success (and what they plan to do about it), you'll gain a lot by being completely honest.

One institution, for example, asked stakeholders what kept the university from achieving greatness. Many of the responses indicated that people on campus tolerated mediocrity and, unless that changed, the institution would never be great. The president and PTF reported this perception back to campus stakeholders so it could be factored into their planning efforts.

7. **Visible and committed senior leadership is essential.** The president has to be seen as supporting, not controlling, the process. If stakeholders believe that the president is engaged with the planning process, they will participate. If they don't see meaningful engagement, they will question the credibility of the entire process. The cabinet or senior team must also support the process. Many of them should serve on the PTF because they will ultimately be charged with implementing it.

8. **High faculty involvement and engagement will make or break the process.** One of the PTF co-chairs must be a highly credibly faculty member, which signals that faculty are helping lead the process and will actively support the plan's implementation. Ideally, 60 percent of the PTF members should be faculty, with other stakeholders making up the remaining 40 percent. This mix communicates to the institution that faculty voices are valued and essential to success.

9. **Avoid the listening-to-ourselves-too-much syndrome.** Everyone on the PTF should pay attention to the external perspective—what is happening nationally and internationally about important issues. They should be well-versed about research trends, technology innovations, student demographics, student and parent expectations, endowment trends, social issues and trends, new teaching strategies, broad financial data, and so forth. Stakeholders need to understand the big picture if they are to craft their own, informed picture for the institution.

10. **Make extraordinary efforts to communicate with stakeholders throughout the planning process and afterward.** When people don't receive accurate and meaningful information, they will not feel valued and will tend to assume the worst. The communication system can use technology effectively, but CSP also requires meaningful face-to-face interaction. Use a variety of communication vehicles, such as president's weekly/monthly e-mail newsletter to the campus, regular Web page updates, and face-to-face meetings.

    Take a "no baloney" approach in which accurate information is openly shared and presented with no hint of a hidden agenda or manipulation. On one campus, the president had the courage to ask for feedback regarding what he could personally do to help the institution move forward. When responding to a survey, about one-third of the task force members indicated that he needed to quit acting like a prima donna and start paying attention to the real issues.

    The survey data shared with the PTF included that finding; because the data were not whitewashed, the president's credibility increased. He also earned points for being open to feedback, committed to learning, and transparent. If the president didn't want to hear the answer, he shouldn't have asked the question. But he did, and the information he received helped him deal with and address pressing institutional issues.

CSP can help create a powerful, motivating, shared picture of the future for any campus that believes in inclusion, shared values, and democratic processes. It takes a special leader to undertake this kind of planning process. Travel safely, and you will have an interesting journey.

RESOURCES

Campus leaders who are interested in collaborative planning may find these additional resources especially helpful.

Axelrod, R.H. (2000) *Terms of Engagement*. San Francisco: Berrett-Koehler

Bossidy, L., & Charan, R. (2000) *Execution: The Discipline of Getting Things Done*. New York: Crown Business

Bunker, B., & Alban, B., (2006) *The Handbook of Large Group Methods*. New York: Jossey-Bass

Holman, P., Devane, T., & Cady, S. (2007) *The Change Handbook*. San Francisco: Berret-Koehler

Jacobs, J. (1997) *Real-Time Strategic Change*. San Francisco: Berrett-Koehler

Napier, R., Sidle, C., Sanaghan, P. (1997) *High Impact Tools and Activities for Strategic Planning*. New York: McGraw-Hill

Sanaghan, P. & Napier, R. (2002) *Intentional Design and The Process of Change*. Washington, D.C.: NACUBO

Senge, P., Kleiner, A., Roberts, C., Roth, G., & Smith, B. (1999) *The Dance of Change*. New York: Doubleday

Weisbord, M. & Janoff, S. (2000) *Future Search*. San Francisco: Barrett-Koehler

Weisbord, M., & Janoff, S. (2007) *Don't Just Do Something, Stand There!* San Francisco: Berrett-Koehler

ADDITIONAL COLLABORATIVE TOOLS

This section provides seven simple, effective tools and techniques that you can use on their own or to support the collaborative designs in this book. All of them enhance collaborative practices by paying attention to group process, neutralizing the impact of overly verbal participants or people with power. All are transparent and focus on outcomes—two important elements of collaborative work.

Constructive Feedback
Level of Difficulty: Easy
Estimated Time: Variable (4 minutes per group presenting)

A collaborative strategic planning process includes many opportunities to present ideas and solicit feedback from stakeholders. Feedback not only helps enhance the ideas but also provides a reality check on their practicality. Unfortunately, some feedback processes turn into "turkey shoots" in which the critics prevail and many ideas (and even people) are destroyed. Instead of being enthused and excited, participants in such meetings leave demoralized and reluctant to attend future presentations.

Higher education tends to value criticism, often under the guise of rigor and discipline. But criticism rarely improves the quality of ideas. The challenge for the collaborative planner is to create a constructive feedback process where criticism has its place but does not become the overriding factor in a discussion of ideas. This technique enables you to obtain effective and honest feedback about a presentation while providing emotional and intellectual safety for the participants. It is most helpful when the trust level within a group is low or when a group member is prone to being critical. This technique collects the ideas of everyone in the room, especially the less verbal ones, and neutralizes the power of the critics.

Logistics

Materials: Large (5" x 7") Post-its (allow 10 to 12 per participant), flipcharts, and easels

Space needs: Large, comfortable room where participants can move around easily

Number of participants: 10 to 50

Facilitator's Directions

Assume that participants have been working in small groups and are ready to present their ideas to the larger group. Before the presentations begin, inform everyone that the feedback process may differ from what they are used to.

— Give each participant 10 or 12 large (5" x 7") Post-it notes on which to write their feedback regarding the presentations. Tell participants that they will have several minutes after each presentation in which to write down their feedback.

— Provide several examples of the desired written feedback, which should address these three elements:

- **What you like about the ideas presented.** For example: "Your idea of having a weekly breakfast meeting for faculty and administrators is just what we need." (Encourage this type of feedback, as people always like to know that others appreciate their ideas.)
- **Resources to share.** This could include people's names, suggested contacts, books, or research that would help leverage or enhance the effectiveness of the suggested ideas or plans presented. For example: "In your plan to assess faculty governance, you should contact Byrne College, which just completed a governance audit" or "You might want to read the article by Dr. Jim Seitz on 'Curriculum Renewal and Faculty Engagement' in the new issue of *Campus Matters.*"
- **Suggestions to improve the ideas presented.** For example: "You suggest that different groups meet with the president regularly. I believe she should visit different places on campus rather than have everyone come to her office" or "Your communication plan seems very one way. You need to build in more interaction where campus stakeholders have the opportunity to provide feedback and ideas."

— For consistency, encourage participants to follow the structured sequence when providing their feedback: 1) things you like about the idea, 2) resources to share, and 3) suggestions for improvement.

— Instruct participants to place the Post-its with their comments on the appropriate flipchart for the presenting group. (Option: You can wait until all the presentations have occurred before placing the Post-its on the flipcharts.)

— Continue the process of presentation, time for written feedback, and placement of Post-its until all the presentations are completed and feedback provided.

— Give each presenting group 15 to 20 minutes to read the notes, react to the feedback, and reach a beginning agreement on how to include the suggestions for improvement and resource ideas, where appropriate.

— If time permits, ask each group to make a brief (two-minute) presentation to the larger group to show how the feedback and suggestions helped influence their thinking.

Las Vegas Voting
Level of Difficulty: Easy
Estimated Time: A Few Minutes

Participative and engaging meetings produce many ideas and suggestions. This, in turn, creates lengthy lists for the group to manage and prioritize. This technique—sometimes referred to as multi-voting—provides a starting point by quickly showing everyone which ideas have top priority. It has the added benefits of being open, democratic, fair, and transparent.

Logistics

Materials: Newsprint, magic markers, sticky dots (found at any stationary or office supply store)

Number of participants: Almost any size group (10 to 100)

Facilitator's Directions

— After the group has developed a list of activities or issues to be prioritized, explain that each participant has five votes to distribute among the ideas on the list. Participants should vote for the ideas they believe will be the best ones to consider and implement. They can weigh their votes in any way; for example, they can place all five votes on one idea, place two votes on one idea and three on another, or vote once for five different ideas.

Before casting any votes, the group may wish to agree on a simple criterion for selecting an idea. For example: It will really make a difference, it's something we could do easily, or it aligns with our culture and tradition.

— Give each participant five sticky dots to place on the flipchart, next to the idea(s) they prefer. If you don't have sticky dots, participants can vote with their fingers: To give a particular idea two votes, they would hold up two fingers. Count the votes as each idea is read aloud and mark the total in view of everyone. Typically, in a few minutes, everyone will have a sense of the top three or four ideas.

If items on a list receive an even number of votes, conduct a second round of voting with three votes per person. This second vote will clarify the priorities because participants can't spread their votes around as much.

> **FACILITATOR'S TIP**
>
> When using Las Vegas Voting, encourage people to use their votes thoughtfully by never giving more than five votes per person. In small groups, three votes per person are plenty.

Mindmapping
Level of Difficulty: Easy
Estimated Time: 30 Minutes

Mindmapping, created and popularized by Tony Buzan in *Use Both Sides of Your Brain* (1983), is the visual depiction of an idea, concept, or issue. It taps both the left and right side of the brain, helping organize information and thought processes without stifling new and different ideas. Use it to

- Stimulate the creative thinking of stakeholders in a meeting
- Diagnose the complexity of a problem or issue
- Capture a lot of ideas and then organize them coherently

Enabling participants to "map" out the complexity of a problem or issue will generate far more ideas than traditional linear listing. It also gives people the opportunity to build on the contributions of others and see connections between ideas they wouldn't see on a long list of brainstormed ideas.

You can use Mindmapping for project planning, defining goals, action planning, note taking, identifying values, or creative problem solving. Everyone's ideas are captured on the Mindmap because all ideas are considered valid and are not judged.

A traditional Mindmap usually limits the ideas created to one word. The adaptation outlined below captures the essence of what people suggest, not just one word, which makes it more productive.

Logistics

Materials: Flipchart paper, colored markers, masking tape

Space needs: A room large enough for participants to move about freely

Number of participants: Up to 50 (If you have more than 50, have two facilitators and two Mindmaps)

Facilitator's Directions

— Tape several sheets of flipchart paper to a wall—the larger the papered area, the better—to form the Mindmap.

— In the center of the Mindmap, state a central theme or problem (for example: How can we further improve campus morale?). Tell participants that the goal is to generate as many ideas as possible to address the focus question or central issue.

— Ask participants to "pair and share"—pair up with the next person and talk about the issue or question to generate ideas and energy.

— After two or three minutes, have participants call out their ideas in a brainstorming fashion. Remember that all ideas are valid, so write down what people say. Print the words on a line and make sure the lines are connected to the major theme in the center. As the ideas are generated, ask participants if the ideas stand by themselves or are part of another idea.

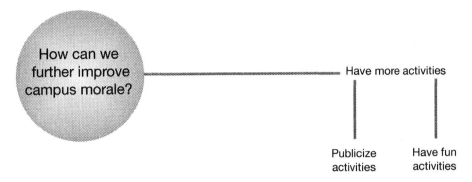

— Use different colors of markers when drawing the Mindmap. Colors stimulate thinking and creativity. You can also use pictures and images to capture an idea. The images don't have to be artistic or beautiful as long as people understand what they represent.

— Continue capturing all the ideas until everyone is finished, then ask participants to observe a minute of silence. After a minute has passed, ask the group if anyone has more ideas. (The minute of silence usually produces several more ideas and might even jumpstart a new series of ideas and connections.)

Your final Mindmap might look like this:

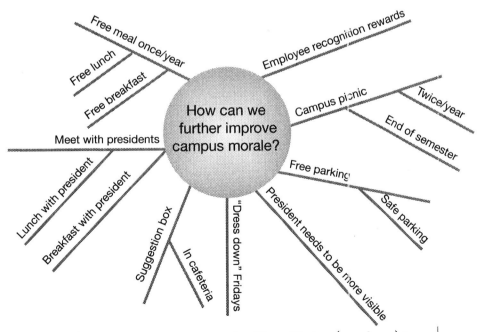

— After completing the Mindmap, you may want to use Las Vegas Voting (see above) to prioritize the ideas. That will enable you to reduce a sizeable number of ideas (30 to 50) to a manageable number (between five and 10).

Nominal Group Technique (NGT)
Level of Difficulty: Easy
Estimated Time: 1 Hour

In any collaborative meeting, the facilitator must remain conscious of group dynamics: Some individuals may find others intimidating (especially if there is a disparity of power), several people may dominate a discussion, the pace and complexity of a discussion can be too fast and overwhelming for some, and shy people might find it challenging to fully participate (especially within an overly verbal group).

This planning technique—developed by Delbecq, Van de Van, and Gustafson in 1971—offers a structured group process for managing these challenges as well as generating and prioritizing ideas, solutions, or recommendations. Use it to
- Solicit the best thinking from meeting participants
- Discuss a sensitive or controversial topic
- Prioritize the ideas that emerge from the group without the undue influence of formal power (president, tenured faculty), overly verbal participants, or strong personalities
- Encourage interaction when the group has a low level of trust

Logistics

Materials: Index cards, flipchart paper, easels, magic markers, pens, and pencils

Space needs: Room large enough for participants to move about freely

Number of participants: 4 to 10

The Nominal Group Technique has seven distinct steps:
1. Define the problem
2. Generate ideas
3. Record the ideas
4. Clarify each idea on the generated list
5. Individually rank items
6. Tally the rankings
7. Hold a wrap-up discussion

Facilitator's Directions

— State the specific problem to be solved or the decision to be made. (For example: What are some ways we can improve the level of trust between our administrators and faculty?)

— Have participants silently generate ideas and suggestions to effectively deal with the focus question. Give them about five or 10 minutes to write their suggestions on an index card. (Limit one suggestion per card.)

— Using a round-robin approach, ask each person to provide one idea at a time. Record all ideas on a flipchart, in full view of everyone, and label each one with a letter of the alphabet. Make as many rounds as necessary until each person has shared all of his or her ideas. If more than one person has the same idea, indicate this with a checkmark (√) rather than listing duplicate ideas.

If the trust level is low in the group, collect the index cards containing the ideas rather than having participants call out their ideas. Give the group a short break while you record the ideas from the index cards on a flipchart. This ensures anonymity while still getting ideas on the table.

At this time, your list may look like this:

A. Have the former president facilitate a meeting between administrators and faculty √

B. Do a climate survey

C. Have the president meet with the faculty senate

D. Have top leaders on both sides participate in a team-building retreat

E. Create a more open decision-making process

F. Share the budget with faculty members √√

G. Do a study on the equity of faculty salaries

H. Create and implement a questionnaire to get at the core issues involved.

I. Use good data

J. Hire a consultant to identify our trust level and issues

K. Find out how other campuses have dealt with this problem

— Make sure everyone understands the suggestions as recorded on the list; no one should judge the ideas or provide feedback on them at this point. Take less than a minute to clarify any item on the list that participants find confusing.

—Tell participants that each of them has five votes. Instruct them to write down the letter corresponding to the idea listed on the flipchart that they wish to vote for. (For example, A = have the former president facilitate a meeting between administrators and faculty and B = do a climate survey). Ask each member to *silently* vote for the best ideas on the long list by assigning them a high number (4 or 5) and to designate their least favorite ideas with a lower number (1 or 2). Remind them they have only five votes overall.

If the list is long (40 ideas or more), use two rounds to vote so participants don't feel overwhelmed. The first round would consider the first 20 items. Then you'd take the remaining 20 ideas and rank them. After you've identified the top ideas from the two rounds, you might find that you still have too many ideas (10 to 12). You might have a third round to choose among the best and identify the top five or six priorities.

— Ask group members to call out their rankings of ideas. List these on a flipchart in full view of everyone. A group's list might look like this:

$$A = 12$$
$$B = 2$$
$$C = 1$$
$$D = 5$$
$$E = 1$$
$$F = 6$$
$$G = 3$$
$$H = 6$$
$$I = 4$$
$$J = 2$$
$$K = 4$$

FACILITATOR'S TIP

If the trust level in the group is low, don't ask participants to call out their rankings of ideas. Instead, collect the individual voting sheets and then tally the results in full view. This way, no one knows who voted for what.

— Have an open discussion about practical next steps for operationalizing the suggestions that received the most votes, including who would have responsibility for implementing them. Keep this discussion to between 15 and 30 minutes.

Self-Managed Groups
Level of Difficulty: Easy

Many times during CSP the large group of participants (20 to 60) will divide into smaller, more manageable groups of five to seven participants. You may give them a specific task, such as, "Please take the next 20 minutes to brainstorm ways to improve communication throughout the campus." Or you might ask the groups to discuss a specific issue, such as, "In the next 45 minutes, please discuss the four recommendations from our self-study on diversity. Be prepared to report back ways to implement the four recommendations." Visiting all the groups to ensure they are using their time well and to resolve any disputes will quickly exhaust the facilitator.

Self-managed groups will leverage the time and productivity of large groups. Use them when:

- Several groups are working simultaneously on a task or a large number of participants in a meeting divide into smaller groups for a meaningful discussion
- You want to provide a structure for groups to accomplish a certain task and be fully responsible for the outcome of their work

Logistics

Materials: Handout explaining the roles

Space needs: Comfortable room where participants can move about freely

Number of participants: 10 to 50 participants

Facilitator's Directions

— Tell participants that each group they form will be self-managing—in other words, responsible for its own work product and process. Note that you won't be checking on them, although you will be available to clarify the task.

— Let all participants know that they need to identify people within their small work groups to take responsibility for one role. This should be done before the group starts work.

— Distribute a handout summarizing the various roles. When assigning a task to a large group to work on in smaller, mixed groups, give them the self-managed handout before they go into their small groups to work.

— Note the roles required by the particular task. You may want to review the various roles and their respective responsibilities, using the following notes for guidance.

- The **Recorder** captures the group's work on the flipchart. You may want to suggest that people assigned to record the group's work don't become trapped in traditional roles. If, for example, the work group includes an administrative assistant or adjunct faculty member, neither should automatically be assigned the role of recorder.
- The **Presenter** shares the small group's work with all participants. Many people will want this high-profile role, but top leaders should avoid it (the campus sees enough of them). Suggest that other people volunteer to serve as the group's presenter.
- The **Timekeeper** gently reminds the group of how much time it has to accomplish the task. About every 10 or 15 minutes, the timekeeper should alert the group to how much time remains. (This is a great role for top leaders, provided they only remind people and don't aggravate them.)
- The **Facilitator** makes sure that all the participants are engaged and involved and that everything remains on track so the group can accomplish the end task. This can involve managing a dominant personality who may start taking over

the group. Because verbal people often volunteer for this role, you might want to deliver this message: "The role of facilitator is challenging. The main purpose is to ensure that everyone in the group participates. If you are doing a lot of talking, you are not facilitating!"

— As participants move into their smaller work groups, remind them to assign the roles right after the entire group has congregated and before any work begins.

Self-Selection
Level of Difficulty: Easy

Self-selection is more of an approach to collaborative work than a specific technique. Its power comes from the idea that if people select the things that they are interested in, rather than being assigned to a particular topic, they will enthusiastically participate and generate better ideas. Use this approach when:

- Stakeholders need to discuss a particular topic so they can understand it better
- Stakeholders need to work on a topic to help solve it, create an action plan, or develop a set of recommendations about it
- You want stakeholders to have the opportunity to work on topics that truly interest them

At times during the CSP process, for example, stakeholders are asked to generate solutions to institutional challenges or to make recommendations on improving a process or a problem. The PTF might find itself addressing issues ranging from faculty governance to residential life, from campus safety to marketing and branding. Each of these complex issues requires the best possible thinking, but how do you ensure that happens? Simply assigning PTF members to a particular topic won't ensure effective participation and generation of ideas.

On the other hand, when people decide for themselves what theme, challenge, or problem they want to work on, they become enthusiastic and produce high-quality ideas. Letting people choose what they want to work on is democratic, treats them like adults, and is a key element in collaborative processes.

FACILITATOR'S TIP

When participants self-select their work groups, you might have two people sign up to work on faculty governance, four on campus safety, and 13 on campus climate. That's exactly how the self-selection is supposed to work. Don't worry about having parity across the topics or try to fix the imbalance by making the groups even. If some topics don't get addressed at the meeting, create another mechanism for those topics to be worked on.

Logistics

Materials: Flipcharts

Space needs: Comfortable room where participants can move about freely

Number of participants: 30 to 40

Facilitator's Directions

— Clarify the meeting's purposes and goals. Say, for example, you have a list of eight major themes that need to be addressed. You might say, "We would like you to spend 30 minutes discussing a theme and generate three recommendations to implement that will help solve/ improve the issue."

— Ask PTF members to select the theme they want to work on in depth. People will vote with their feet and quickly show where their interests lie. If you have eight topics, for instance, you may find that four or five attract the most attention from participants.

— Once the groups have organized around a particular theme, remind participants to assign roles (see above) to help their group work effectively.

Parking Lot
Level of Difficulty: Easy

In high-energy meetings, smart, energized participants often wander away from the original purpose or the agreed-upon agenda. Suddenly, participants may find themselves discussing an idea or issue that has nothing to do with the meeting. Then they may mumble, "What's going on here? Why are we talking about course scheduling when we are here to talk about limited parking on campus?"

Once a group wanders off, you may find it difficult to get everyone back on track. This is especially true when the group includes strong egos, a revered participant, or a respected leader. What can a student possibly say when the provost takes the discussion in a different direction from the meeting's purpose?

This time-tested technique, sometimes called the Grasscatcher, captures the important yet off-topic ideas rather than letting them take the group off on a tangent. Quite simply, this technique "parks" tangential ideas on a sheet of flipchart paper so participants can return to them after completing the task at hand. It's particularly useful for groups that meet regularly, such as administrative councils, technology groups, or faculty senate.

Logistics

Materials: Flipcharts and magic markers

Space needs: A room large enough for participants to move about freely

Number of participants: 16 to 20

Facilitator's Directions

— Confirm the general purpose of the meeting before it begins. Say, for example, "Today, we are working on improving campus morale" or "The primary purpose of this meeting is to prepare for the large planning conference we're having next week."

— Let participants know that you will be using a Parking Lot design to capture important ideas that may arise during in the meeting but have little to do with its stated purpose. For example: "Our purpose is to find ways to improve campus morale. We don't want to ignore a particular problem that may come up about a dorm, but that problem doesn't fit with the purpose of the meeting. So we will capture the dorm problem on a flipchart and, before we leave, agree upon a next step for it."

— Emphasize that the Parking Lot issues will be addressed and not forgotten. Be sure to leave at least 15 minutes toward the end of the meeting to address any issues in the Parking Lot.

Say, for example, two unrelated issues came up during a meeting about campus morale.

As recorded by the facilitator, the Parking Lot might look like this:

Issue: The physical plant people have reported a leak in St. Patrick's Hall

Action: John will talk with the physical plant director and come up with a plan by tomorrow

Issue: The campus newsletter isn't being distributed to all the divisions

Action: Mary will contact our communication director this afternoon to validate this claim and solve the problem by the end of the week.

EXECUTIVE SUMMARY OF THE COLLABORATIVE STRATEGIC PLANNING PROCESS

Collaborative Strategic Planning (CSP) is a highly engaging process that's both inclusive in nature and efficient in execution. The five-phase process is designed to create commitment for the implementation of the strategic plan from the very start of planning. A highly credible internal Planning Task Force drives the entire process, which taps into and builds the capacity of the institution to think and plan collaboratively. Campus stakeholders feel heard and valued as their meaningful involvement helps create a bright future for the institution.

Numerous higher education institutions, including Saint Joseph's University, Bellarmine University, and The University of the West Indies, have effectively implemented CSP. It has also been used in a statewide strategic planning process in Pennsylvania and with several nonprofit organizations.

Guiding Principles

To be successful, the process depends on five guiding principles.

1. Meaningful engagement of institutional stakeholders—through face-to-face interaction and discussion—is at the heart of collaborative planning.
2. Transparency is essential. Information gathered throughout the planning process is shared with everyone.
3. The role of the consultant or facilitator is to help tap into and build the capacity of the internal stakeholders and guide the planning process, not direct it.
4. The process pays attention to the external issues and trends in higher education so that institutional stakeholders don't become too inwardly focused.
5. At several points, the planning process engages external stakeholders, such as alumni, community leaders, and businesspeople. Their inclusion helps create a well-informed plan that intelligently responds to the pace and complexity of change and to different stakeholder interests.

Timeline

Here is a general timeline of the collaborative planning process; in total, the five phases typically take one year to complete:

Phase I: Getting Organized	2 months
Phase II: Data Gathering and Engagement	3 months
Phase III: Making Sense of the Issues	2–3 months
Phase IV: Vision Conference	1–2 months
Phase V: Goals Conference	1–2 months

Phase I: Getting Organized

Good beginnings are essential to the success of the collaborative strategic planning process. Therefore, the president must ensure that an effective and efficient planning process takes place by:

- Communicating to the campus that strategic planning is important to the future of the institution and showing genuine interest and enthusiasm for an inclusive, participative, and transparent process. This has to be done throughout the process and not just at the beginning.
- Committing the technological resources to the planning process to ensure that everyone knows how to be involved, can contribute ideas and feedback to the process, and remains fully informed through periodic updates.
- Clarifying his or her role in the planning process as a champion and supporter but not a driver or controller.
- Visibly and authentically supporting the process by attending training sessions, communicating with the diverse stakeholder groups throughout the campus about the process, and—most important—listening to people's concerns and aspirations.
- Establishing a highly credible strategic Planning Task Force (PTF).

The PTF is both a thinking and a doing group. Ideally, it should number between 20 and 30 and have two co-chairs—preferably one faculty member and one high-level administrator. Initial responsibilities of the task force include establishing a calendar of events for the year, developing a communication plan, identifying forums for engagement and data gathering (such as faculty senate meetings and staff and administrative councils) and learning about collaborative planning and meeting designs that engage stakeholders' thinking and passions.

Phase II: Data Gathering and Engagement

At the heart of collaborative planning is the meaningful engagement of stakeholders throughout the institution. Engagement means face-to-face interaction, discussion, and dialogue. Surveys have a secondary role in collaborative planning.

The planning process begins with a two-day training for all task force members, during which a consultant shares a variety of highly interactive planning activities. Each activity not only generates data from PTF members but also teaches them how to use the activity to engage with other stakeholders throughout the institution. A Stakeholder Review provides a clear picture of who needs to be connected to and informed about the planning process as it moves forward.

When the training concludes, task force members are prepared to work in pairs to engage faculty, staff, administrators, and external stakeholders. Building the capacity of the task force members to implement the collaborative planning process has several benefits:

- The task force members "own" the process because they are at the heart of it
- Internal stakeholders witness their peers and colleagues working hard to create an effective planning process
- The credibility of the planning process increases because it is led by insiders and not by outsiders
- Task force members develop the expertise to do collaborative planning in their own departments and administrative units
- The institution saves money because insiders, not consultants, do most of the work

Phase III: Making Sense of the Issues

After the PTF has conducted dozens of interactive meetings throughout the campus, the great deal of information generated goes into a centralized database. At this stage, the PTF spends a full day reporting out their findings. PTF members also select between five and eight strategic themes to help focus the planning process (such as academic excellence, diversity, and the role of research).

Next, PTF members form teams to write concept papers, which describe the strategic themes and their importance to the institution. These papers distill the information gathered during the data-gathering phase into more manageable chunks so stakeholders can become informed about the issues without being deluged by information. The concept papers, which run approximately five pages, provide historical context for the issues; identify regional, national, and international perspectives about the issues; and describe how campus stakeholders see the issues, based on the data gathering that has taken place.

All concept papers are reviewed by task force members before being shared with the community at large via the campus intranet. During the writing of the concept papers, in-depth discussion and debate occur between PTF members. When the final concept papers are produced, the PTF members clearly own the information.

Phase IV: Vision Conference

This highly interactive, one-day meeting involves 50 to 75 stakeholders. (A large institution would have several one-day vision conferences rather than one with 100 or more participants.) It is not a "blue sky" brainstorming session but is grounded in quality information and institutional realities.

Sixty percent of the attendees are internal stakeholders (all PTF members attend) and 40 percent are external. The external stakeholders—such as alumni, community businesspeople, and neighborhood leaders—provide a broader and unique perspective as the participants envision the institution's future.

The Vision Conference has three distinct elements:

Review of Concept Papers and Discussion. All conference participants have a chance to review the concept papers and glean the essential themes from each one. This helps ensure that all participants are well-informed about the institutional issues before they think about the future of the institution. Reviewing the concept papers creates a shared experience and database for participants and helps set the stage for creating a preferred future.

Stakeholder Review. This involves the different stakeholders attending the Vision Conference (such as faculty, students, businesspeople, and community leaders) organizing themselves and discussing their view of the institution's future. Based on its unique stakeholder perspective, each group shares four or five key themes with the entire group. Sharing the different perspectives expands participants' thinking, creates the opportunity to understand what is important to others, and develops a deeper pool of ideas.

Creating a Preferred Future. The conference culminates with an exercise to create shared pictures of the future. Participants work in small, diverse groups and envision the future based on a five-year horizon. If diversity is a strategic theme, for example, participants would describe what diversity looks like on campus five years from now.

After each small group shares its preferred future with the whole group, a facilitated discussion identifies the common ground and recurrent themes. Campus leaders use these elements to draft a vision statement for the institution that then goes to internal stakeholders for review and refinement. The Planning Task Force usually appoints a small group to draft a vision statement and take responsibility for incorporating the feedback received into a final version.

Phase V: Goals Conference

Approximately one month after the Vision Conference, the Planning Task Force convenes for one or two days to create a broad implementation plan for the institution. At this time, other stakeholders outside of the PTF are invited to lend their expertise and energy to creating the goals. Often, these are the people who will be charged with implementing the strategic plan.

Participants use the new vision statement to create a set of goals for each strategic theme (such as diversity, academic excellence, and research). After agreeing upon the strategic goals, participants create action plans for each one. Feedback processes built into the conference ensure that all participants share their advice and ideas when creating the action plans.

The draft action plan usually goes to the president's cabinet for discussion and review. It typically takes another four to six weeks to produce a detailed implementation plan.

IMPLEMENTATION PLAN

GOALS CONFERENCE(S)
Task Force Members
Relevant Insiders

VISION CONFERENCE(S)
External Allies and Stakeholders
Key Internal Stakeholders
Task Force

**UNDERSTANDING THE ISSUES/
SENSE MAKING**
Reading Data from Interactive Meetings
Research and Discussion
Concept Papers Created

DATA GATHERING & ENGAGEMENT
External Perspective Critical
Variety of Engagements
1 to 1 Interviews
Focus Groups
Surveys
Large Interactive Meetings

PLANNING & GETTING ORGANIZED
Stakeholder Review Conducted
Calendar Organized
Task Force Members Identified
Task Force Training

SAMPLE CONCEPT PAPER: ACADEMICS

Background

Central to the identity of Incredible University is the quality and effectiveness of its academic programs. Building on this accepted premise, we reviewed our academic program, summarizing our achievements and what we have learned since 2004. Our analysis addresses five key sections: curriculum and programs, outcomes assessment, international and diversity issues, academic support services, and faculty personnel issues.

Undergraduate and Graduate Curricular Programs

Incredible University introduced new general education requirements in the fall of 2004 semester that apply to both the Women's College and Adult Undergraduate Degree Program student populations. After several years, it is time to revisit the nature and purpose of the general education requirement and determine if it serves the mission of the college and contemporary needs.

Several other undergraduate curricular initiatives have been undertaken in these years, based on institutional strengths and in response to students' and societal needs. New programs introduced during this time include majors in International Studies, American Studies, Justice Studies, Individualized Special Majors, Biochemistry, and Applied Science, plus minors in Women's Studies and Political Science.

These are all interdisciplinary programs initiated and developed by faculty with input from students, consultants, and internal committees. Majors in Communications, Foods and Nutrition, and Religious Studies were introduced in the Adult Undergraduate Degree Program. Several departments, including Business Administration and History, engaged in a review/revision of their curricula.

In response to an awareness of our need to prepare students for living in a globally interdependent world, we have added courses in Caribbean Culture, International Nursing, Japanese, and Chinese. Similarly, to this end, policies have been developed to encourage and enable students to study abroad and undertake internships.

The Graduate Program, with its cutting-edge core curriculum, has been an area of major academic activity during these years. In 1994–95 we began our first graduate program, a master's degree in Education: Human Services Leadership. Today, the university offers master's degrees in several areas. Additions include: Educational Technology, Nutrition, Counseling Psychology, Theology, Management/Leadership, and Health Care Management.

An innovative program in Business Administration enables students to complete both a bachelor's and a master's degree in five years. We are now at a point in the Graduate Program's growth where we need to assess its organization, its future directions, and its relationship to the Adult Undergraduate Degree Program.

Since 1980, The Center for Theological and Spiritual Development has conducted a dynamic, fast-growing, and nationally recognized Summer Institute Program. Renowned faculty has come to campus to conduct courses on the graduate and undergraduate levels to help the university advance its mission.

Technology has been integrated in the curriculum in a variety of ways in all programs, and faculty development has been offered to facilitate this integration. Specific information on this area appears in the Technology Concept Paper.

Academic Outcomes Assessment

A top priority in reference to ongoing curriculum is the development of an outcomes assessment plan. Such a plan enables the various academic departments to ascertain their areas of strength and weakness and thereby engage in serious academic planning to ensure continued effectiveness.

In 2000 the Vice President for Academic Affairs appointed an Academic Outcomes Assessment Committee, consisting of faculty and administrators from all programs, to develop a plan and implementation strategy. The committee has worked steadily and effectively over the past several years and has made solid progress. After many meetings, workshops, and individualized consultations, each academic department has developed a mission statement, goals and objectives, and a curriculum map for assessing how it is achieving its stated goals and objectives. An outcomes assessment plan still needs to be developed for the undergraduate general education program—a challenging and vital task.

International Programs and Diversity

Incredible University has a serious commitment to the education of international students, both for their benefit and the benefit of the American students. Most international students are enrolled in the Women's College; however, some are in the Adult Undergraduate Degree Program and in the Graduate Program.

The university recognizes the need for support services for this cohort and continues to examine ways to serve them better. New academic initiatives in recent years have included several new ESL courses, a course on The American Classroom, and a concentration in the English major (English Language for International Students). Many international students avail themselves of the tutoring and workshops that the college has funded specifically for them. The Director of ESL and the International Student Advisor are significant support personnel and regularly interact with faculty to monitor the students' academic progress.

The value of diversity is constantly recognized, and several academic areas are specifically charged to realize its potential. In addition to curricular offerings, the college has two undergraduate programs that embrace academic areas related to diversity: the Hispanic Leadership Program (HLP) and the Educational Opportunity Fund (EOF). The directors of both of these programs, while having specific programs for the enrolled students, are eager to integrate the students into existing programs rather than isolate them. Each program is constantly reviewing its goals and objectives; each is to provide programs for all students that reflect important cultural knowledge and understanding. Among these are roundtable discussions on pressing Latina issues and presentations highlighting unity through the arts.

Academic Support Services

The staff of Byrne Library has continued to work closely with the academic departments and programs to enhance the delivery of quality library services. As new undergraduate majors and graduate programs are developed, the library has endeavored to meet their needs as well as those of existing programs. As nontraditional-aged and part-time students have increased, the library has been challenged to change and expand the delivery of its services to meet their needs. The library has endeavored, within the limits of its staff, to change/expand its hours of services. Two means of increasing the library's resources have been to develop cooperative arrangements with other local libraries and to use technological resources (covered in the Technology Concept Paper).

The Resource Learning Center is the major provider of academic support services. In recent years, the center has restructured the academic skills courses it offers and placed an emphasis on effective learning strategies. These changes serve not only the needs of our Women's College students but also our entire student population. A variety of workshops on study skills are offered each semester for students in all programs. Tutoring, at no charge, is offered to all. There is continuous dialogue between the director of the Learning Center and faculty members as students use these services. This is important as we endeavor to increase retention rates. The location of the center does not render it readily accessible. Plans to relocate are being made.

Faculty Personnel Issues

Critical to the success of the academic enterprise is a qualified, committed faculty. The university is indeed fortunate to have such a group. As we advance academically, we are keenly aware of our responsibility to address faculty needs.

In recent years, ongoing faculty development has been advanced in several ways. Periodic faculty development workshops are held on campus. A release-time grant program has been initiated to enable faculty to devote time to scholarly productivity. In 1994–95 there were 96 full-time instructor faculty; in 2006–07 there were 137. In 2000, a task force was formed to address the issue of faculty salaries. As a result, the university has developed a five-year plan whereby salaries will be adjusted to be at the AAUP 80th percentile level for our Carnegie Classification. Workload issues are under consideration.

Lessons Learned

A review of academic activity in the past years clearly indicates that we are, and will be, impacted by change. External competition, changing student bodies, changing societal needs, emphasis on continuing education, and technological advances all tell us ongoing change is a constant. Accordingly, ongoing assessment is critical.

We must constantly identify new markets and new modalities of delivery. We will need to enter into more articulation agreements and partnerships, offer courses/degree programs off-site, and further integrate technology into the learning environment. Learning will take place on different fronts, virtually around the clock. We will also need to procure new sources of funding (such as grants) and foster faculty development. Creativity and risk taking will be important as we continue to fulfill our mission for academic excellence in a changing world.

Trends in Higher Education

- In New Jersey, the number of high school students graduating between 2005 and 2011 is anticipated to rise 18 percent
- In the years 2005–2015 it is expected that there will be a 19 percent growth in college students, of whom 80 percent will be minority
- In 2008, 40 percent of students will be adult and 57 percent will be female

Projected growth markets:

Students of color
Commuters
Part-time students
Older students

Given that the average person is expected to change careers five or six times in his/her lifetime, the educational system will likely change. There will be a continued need for education, including the values context provided by liberal arts and a general education curriculum. It is uncertain whether that need will be recognized in a system that concentrates increasingly on costs per se. Recognition of higher education is apt to be more significantly gained by linking its mission to the public agenda as a positive source in addressing societal needs and proactively partnering in the betterment of society.

There will also be the need for education for change/career change at those critical points in the person's lifetime. Such education will concentrate on specific skills or competencies rather than the liberal arts. Connected with this and the rise of distance education, emphasis on "seat time" and credits will decline dramatically.

There will be a need for enrichment courses and programs for people who wish to develop a talent and don't care—and won't pay—for credit courses. In connection with this, degrees as such will become less important while certifications of specific knowledge or skills will become more important.

The development of distance education has a number of implications:

- In addition to the existing courses and programs via distance education, many entire degree programs are drawing a number of students.
- Colleges will have to enter the distance education field in some manner to survive. This may mean delivering academic programs only in a distance education mode, providing distance education for their own students and possibly others, becoming brokers in that they no longer produce all the courses themselves but find alternative sources to teach some courses via distance education, or certifying course work done elsewhere.
- As courses and programs become increasingly available through nontraditional sources, the need for full-time faculty will change and roles may change. A "star system" will likely develop, with nationally known faculty taking on larger roles and local faculty diminishing or changing in their roles by serving increasingly as mentors and advisors while still teaching.
- As students become more used to, and demanding of, anytime/anywhere education, the way in which we do business—not only the teaching but also the advising, registering, and other functions—will have to become more flexible as well.
- Corporations have already entered the education field. Some of them farm out programs to traditional institutions of higher education; some of them have actually become accredited, degree-granting institutions.

Strategic Themes for the Future

The issue of the glass ceiling for women is not quite what it was in the past. The concept of the nurturing environment that characterizes this university can easily be extended to everyone (male, female, and the increasingly diverse population that is developing).

As a value-centered Catholic college in the liberal arts tradition, we are engaged in educating the whole person for a meaningful place in the world. To do so we will need to:

- Ensure appropriate resource allocation in light of our mission and emerging trends
- Increase institutional agility to accommodate change efficiently and effectively
- Use outcomes assessment results as a basis for decision making
- Identify internal and external opportunities for collaboration and cooperation in program development
- Identify competitors and respond appropriately

- Develop a more user-friendly/student-centered community environment to foster the academic enterprise
- Adapt to an emerging 24/7 institutional model
- Increase faculty development to support the changing academic roles

SAMPLE CONCEPT PAPER: VISIBILITY

Introduction and Background

Over the past 10 years Incredible University's academic growth, changes in leadership, and historical milestones have provided opportunities for the university to become more visible in its immediate environs. Since 2001, at least seven new undergraduate degree programs were added and a thriving graduate program established and nurtured. During this time, programs offered to nontraditional-age undergraduates were consolidated under a new name, creating a new associate dean's position.

In 2003 the governance structure of the university was reorganized, creating a five-member cabinet to work with the president; a new president was inaugurated in July 2005. The university celebrated its 100th anniversary with 12 months of public and campus events, including a mention on national television. In 2006, completion of a long-awaited renovation project—Seitz Hall and its attendant greenhouse and garden—has further shone a spotlight on the university.

During this same time, the university budget devoted to visibility has grown dramatically. Advertising and publications, under the direction of the Office of Communications and Marketing, have become more unified and professional, more numerous, and more expensive. Most of the budget has been focused on print media, with a lesser amount devoted to radio, billboards, or cable television.

The university's Web site, developed in house for a minimal cost, has remained essentially unchanged since its inception in 1997. Although regularly updated with new events and information, the Web site is underused as a communications and recruitment medium.

While the resources devoted to advertising and publications have increased, enrollment has shrunk or remained level, except for graduate degree programs. At the same time, many university staff perceive that the university lacks appropriate visibility within the local and larger environs, usually attested to by a shortage of newspaper articles about the university. The general feeling is that "nobody knows we're here."

All of these factors indicate a need to rethink the way the university applies resources to promote its visibility. The university faces the challenge of marketing several diverse programs to discrete audiences in one of the most expensive commercial markets in the world—metropolitan New York. The same challenge is present in competing for news coverage when there is a shortage of local news outlets and a bias toward "big city" news.

Despite a pale media presence, the university enjoys a solid academic standing among professional peers, as evidenced by its accreditation record and uncommonly positive Middle States reviews. Its reputation in preparing excellent teachers is well-recognized regionally. A number of its faculty and students have, to their credit, outstanding publications, presentations, professional honors, or other recognitions that add to the university's stature. Respected lecturers and performers visit the campus, although their presence should be better noted, both internally and externally.

Lessons Learned

The lessons to be taken from the past 10 years are several:

Spend the money to do things right. Although costly, the elegant centennial celebrations powerfully and effectively built pride in the past and confidence in the future among alumnae/i, faculty, staff, and the general public. Coupled with the capital campaign, these public events have been seen publicly as the engine moving the university energetically into its next stage as a center of academic achievement.

Build on strengths. The rapid growth of the Graduate Degree program since 1994 dramatizes how success breeds success. Beginning with the university's strongest undergraduate degree programs—and those with the largest alumnae/i bases—the Graduate Program continues to increase in enrollment as other divisions struggle to keep up. This program also tapped into a ready and waiting market of teachers and nurses ready to progress to post-graduate degrees. Its unique multi-disciplinary core design is seen as consistent with the university's mission and as a valuable approach to higher education.

Take bold steps. Visible improvements to campus over the past two years, including the administration building renovation, send unmistakable messages to internal and external audiences. Upgrades in technology, beautification projects, repairs to roof and heating systems, improved signage, air conditioning, floor resurfacing, and room painting—along with the dramatic renewal of Seitz Hall—impress residents, commuters, employees, and visitors alike.

Plan and coordinate a marketing plan. Each year the university's advertising is scheduled six to months in advance to promote open houses, registration, and other important events for each recruiting division. However, the lack of a cohesive, 18- to 24-month marketing plan has proven a drawback for the entire university. Rather than following a disciplined and well-conceived plan, the university has sometimes reacted to low enrollment predictions with stop-gap measures, usually without much success.

The strategies, schedule, leadership, and areas of responsibility for a marketing plan must be clearly set out and roles defined to make it effective. To this end, the university's marketing committee, composed of the Dean of Admission, Associate Deans of Graduate and Adult Undergraduate Degree Programs, and the Director of Communications and Marketing, as well as the president, should be reactivated.

Plan and coordinate a visibility plan. A second 18- to 24-month visibility plan is also needed. This more comprehensive plan includes marketing efforts as well as media relations, event planning and scheduling, image advertising, strategic dissemination of print materials to persons of influence, community outreach, civic and legislative activism, alumnae/i relations, and relations with the business community. Chief among these tasks is aggressive placement of stories and opinion pieces in the media, coupled with strategic planning of campus events to correspond to media schedules and topics of interest.

Make internal communications a priority. Our best advertising is word of mouth. Our best salespersons are the students, faculty, and staff who are here already. Keeping these people well-informed empowers them, keeps them connected to the mission and goals of the university, and helps them communicate that news outside.

Keep it simple. Clever acronyms or double-entendres, such as CAST, AUDP, or Intersession, may prevent people from clearly and readily understanding the university's messages. To have the widest possible visibility, the words must be understandable by the widest possible audience.

National Trends

Nationally, the immediacy and ease of interactive electronic communications have changed the way of doing business, even for educational institutions. The Web has become the major marketing tool for colleges, and campus technology itself is a major selling point in attracting new students.

Online courses, coupled with other distant learning delivery modes, will continue to proliferate. Some of the university's competitors far outspend it, both in campus technology and advertising/publications.

Strategic Themes

Several strategic themes for this university's visibility stem from these background lessons and national trends:

- Image/identity as a liberal arts university with co-educational graduate and undergraduate programs for students from all over the country
- Role of fine and performing arts within the holistic learning experience of a liberal arts education
- Expansion of academic programs to increase electronic course delivery and increase certificate/non-credit programs
- Celebration and communication of strengths, especially faculty and student achievements

Short-Term Tasks

In the short term, several tasks can be undertaken to improve visibility:

- Revive the Marketing Committee
- Write 18- to 24-month marketing and visibility plans that incorporate electronic as well as traditional communication modes
- Review publications for cost-saving effectiveness
- Redesign the university Web site to be more inclusive, accessible, and powerful for all constituencies

Long-Term Tasks

Long range tasks to improve visibility include:

- Maintain a competitive, vibrant Web site; invest in making it the best in the region
- Focus on faculty and student achievements; celebrate on-campus/publicize off-campus
- Coordinate and improve promotion of special events
- Improve internal communications dramatically
- Promote public usage of facilities as an income-producing activity

SAMPLE PLANNING AUDIT

Before engaging in its work, the Planning Task Force (PTF) should have some sense of the institution's capacity to plan effectively and collaboratively. You may conduct this informal survey as part of the two-day training session for PTF members in Phase I (see Chapter 2). Then you could tabulate the results and share them with PTF members either during the training session or soon afterward at a breakfast or lunch meeting. The survey data should go directly to the president and PTF co-chairs for review before being presented to the task force.

Have each member of the PTF take the survey anonymously to ensure honest answers. This survey is informal and not meant to be statistically valid. Its main purpose is to capture and convey information helpful to the leaders of the institution and the task force as they think about and organize their collaborative planning process.

Conducting the survey will:

- Provide valuable information about and insight into your institution's capacity to plan. This will make you smarter about your institution from the beginning of the planning process. Most campuses are unaware of their current capacity to plan collaboratively, so you will jumpstart the process by being consciously aware of your strengths and weaknesses.

- Use the PTF as a strategic asset. Members' opinions and perspectives will inform the creation and design of the planning process.

- Model both transparency and courage. The results must be reported back to the PTF members even if—and especially if—they point to difficulties or raise tough questions to address. This honesty underscores the integrity of the entire planning process.

Planning Audit

1. How would you rate the quality of communication throughout the campus?

1	**2**	**3**	**4**	**5**	**6**	**7**	**8**	**9**	**10**
Very Poor				Average					Excellent

2. How do you rate the commitment of the senior management team, including the president, to doing collaborative strategic planning?

1	**2**	**3**	**4**	**5**	**6**	**7**	**8**	**9**	**10**
No Commitment				Average Commitment					Very High Commitment

3. How do you rate the organization's ability to collect meaningful information from its stakeholders?

1	**2**	**3**	**4**	**5**	**6**	**7**	**8**	**9**	**10**
No Ability At All				Average Ability					Excellent Ability

4. How would you rate the quality of the decisions made by the cabinet in moving the institution forward?

1	**2**	**3**	**4**	**5**	**6**	**7**	**8**	**9**	**10**
Very Poor				Average Quality					Excellent Quality

5. How would you rate the effectiveness of past planning efforts?

1	**2**	**3**	**4**	**5**	**6**	**7**	**8**	**9**	**10**
Not Effective				Somewhat Effective					Very Effective

6. How would you rate the institution's willingness to ask tough questions? (For example: What are our weaknesses as an institution? How would you describe the quality of our senior leadership group? What gets in the way of us achieving excellence)?

1	2	3	4	5	6	7	8	9	10
Not Very Willing				Somewhat Willing					Very Willing

7. How would you describe the level of collaboration across the institution?

1	2	3	4	5	6	7	8	9	10
Non-Existent				We Collaborate At Times					Very High Level of Collaboration

8. How do you rate the institution's internal ability to plan effectively? (For example: Do we have good facilitators, people with the ability to make sense out of complex data, and good information-gathering practices?)

1	2	3	4	5	6	7	8	9	10
Very Low				Average Ability					Very High Ability

9. How would you rate our ability to execute and get things done as an institution?

1	2	3	4	5	6	7	8	9	10
Very low Execution Skills				Average Execution Skills					High Execution Skills

10. How would you rate our ability to measure performance toward stated goals?

1	2	3	4	5	6	7	8	9	10
Very Low				Average					Very High

11. As we embark on an institution-wide planning process, what advice or recommendations do you have for the president?

notes